Bernard Shaw on Cinema

Edited and with an Introduction by

Bernard F. Dukore

Bernard Shaw on Cinema

Southern Illinois University Press ◆ Carbondale and Edwardsville

Title page illustration: Luncheon party in Marion Davies's bungalow on the MGM lot, Culver City, 1933. *Left to right:* Charlie Chaplin, Shaw, Davies, Louis B. Mayer, Clark Gable, George Hearst. Sidney P. Albert Collection, Brown University Library.

Library of Congress Cataloging-in-Publication Data

Shaw, George Bernard, 1856–1950.
    Bernard Shaw on cinema / edited and with an introduction by Bernard F. Dukore.
            p.   cm.
Includes bibliographical references and index.
    1. Motion pictures.   I. Dukore, Bernard Frank, 1931–
II. Title.
PN1994.S5183   1997
791.43—DC21   97-19680
ISBN 0-8093-2154-8 (alk. paper)   CIP
ISBN 0-8093-2155-6 (pbk. : alk. paper)

Contents

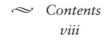

Acknowledgments

FOR THEIR HELP in making this book possible, I am extremely happy to express my gratitude to Dan H. Laurence, who has generously made many Shavian documents available to me and who has helped my understanding of Shaw in many ways, and to Roma Woodnutt, of the Society of Authors, who has provided common sense and encouragement when both were needed.

For their kindness in providing otherwise inaccessible items for this book, I am beholden to Sidney P. Albert, Valerie Pascal Delacorte, and Rhoda Nathan. I also appreciate Tom and Frances Evans for their explanation of old-fashioned British slang.

I should not fail to recognize with gratitude Virginia Tech, the popular and affectionate nickname of Virginia Polytechnic Institute and State University, for its enlightened assistance to scholars and scholarship, chiefly through released time to do research and to write, but also for the ambience it has created by its University Distinguished Professorships.

Acknowledgments are also due to certain persons and archives for permission to examine and print manuscripts: Dan H. Laurence, for postal cards from Shaw to Cecil Lewis (9 Aug. 1933) and Marjorie Deans (13 Oct. 1941) and for letters from Shaw to Marjorie Deans (25 Jan. 1941, 3 Aug. 1943); Valerie Pascal Delacorte, for letters from Shaw to Gabriel Pascal (18 Nov. 1946) and Ercole Graziadei (24 Jan. 1950) and for the standard Shaw license to film one of his plays; Sidney P. Albert Collection, Brown University Library, for a note from Shaw to Rex Ingram; Harry Ransom Humanities Research Center, the University of Texas at Austin, for letters from Shaw to Arthur W. Pinero (12 Dec. 1908) and William Lestocq (19 Feb. 1919); Fales Manuscript Collection,

Fales Library, New York University, for a letter from Shaw to Horace Liveright (7 May 1920); and the British Library, for a letter from Shaw to Mr. Messulam (Add. MS 50522).

Let me take this opportunity to thank Southern Illinois University Press's anonymous readers of the manuscript for their valuable suggestions.

Introduction

It ought to be the first endeavour of a writer to distinguish
nature from custom; or that which is established because it is
right, from that which is right only because it is established.
                                        —Samuel Johnson, *Rambler*

ON 22 MARCH 1895, at the Society for the Encouragement of National
Industry in Paris, the Lumière brothers, Louis and Auguste, demonstrated
the cinematograph, which projected motion pictures on a screen. Later
that year, they showed moving pictures to a paying public, as did Max
and Emil Skladanowsky in Berlin; but four years earlier, Shaw was primed
to appreciate silent movies. On 8 April 1891, in his music column of the
World, he admitted that

> on the chance occasions when I descend from the opera house
> to the theatre I am often made to feel acutely that the play would
> be much more enjoyable if the dialogue were omitted. To me, the
> popular dramatist always appears as a sympathetic, kindly, emo-
> tional creature, able to feel and to imagine in a pleasantly simple
> and familiar groove, but almost destitute of intellect, and therefore
> unable to think or to write. When he is merely emotioning he is
> the best of good company for an easygoing hour of sentimental
> relaxation; but the moment he opens his mouth he becomes
> insufferable.[1]

The quotation is from a review of *L'Enfant Prodigue*, a pantomime
that employed conventional ballet and melodramatic music. "I was
touched when I laughed no less than when I retired in tears at the end
of the third act," wrote Shaw. "But my emotion was not caused by the
music," which he adversely criticized. "For the rest of this most entertain-

ing dumb show I have nothing but praise" (306–7). Yet he kept his perspective:

> In estimating the value of these eulogies, it must be remembered that although the satisfaction of seeing a simple thing consummately well done is most joyful and soothing after a long and worrying course of complex things imperfectly done, the simple success must not therefore be placed above the complex half success. A drama consisting of a series of emotions, so obvious in their sequence that they can be made intelligible to a general audience by pure phenomena is child's play compared to ordinary drama, or opera, although no actor can venture upon it without a degree of skill in pantomime which most speakers and singers think (erroneously) that they can afford to do without. (308–9)

Shaw's views of silent films resembled his view of *L'Enfant Prodigue*. Although he valued what was admirable, he recognized that there were types and degrees of excellence.

He was an avid moviegoer. He was familiar with the acting of Max Linder, Charlie Chaplin, and Mary Pickford. On his travels, if he had a few free hours and a movie were playing, in he went. When Ivor Montagu and others organized the Film Society in 1925 to show intrinsically meritorious films unavailable for viewing in commercial movie houses, Shaw was among its first guarantors, and he sometimes dropped into its screening rooms for viewings.[2] In the thirties and forties, he continued moviegoing. His engagement diary for his ninety-first birthday, 26 July 1947, which he spent at his home in the village of Ayot St. Lawrence, records, "Films at Rectory Cottage."[3] His admission, "I am very fond of the movies. I am what they call in America 'a movie fan,'" was accurate ("[Beauty But No Sex Appeal]," 18 November 1927).[4]

He made fun of his own interest in cinema—"the damned thing is such an irresistible toy that it fascinates the boy in me" ("[The Writer and the Film Industry]," 12 December 1908)—but he did not belittle it: "I, who go to an ordinary theatre with effort and reluctance, cannot

keep away from the cinema" ("[Shaw's Fascination with the Movies],"
19 August 1912). Moviemakers reciprocated his interest. As early as
1908, the first selection in this book reveals, he was asked to write original silent film scenarios. By 1913, he exclaimed, "I am up to my neck in
cinematic proposals!"[5] In 1919, Samuel Goldwyn offered a thousand
pounds in advance of either 15 percent of the gross or a third of the
profits for an original screenplay.[6] By 1921, offers of ten thousand
pounds for film rights to one of his plays were standard ("[Taxation
and Windfall Income from Films]," 16 March 1921).

Far earlier than most people, Shaw foresaw that moviemaking would
become organized "on the biggest modern scale, by a bloated trust" and
that leagues of authors should formulate model contracts for their members ("[The Writer and the Film Industry]," 12 December 1908). He
regarded the economic aspect of moviemaking in exactly the term
employed by moviemakers themselves, an industry. Like every industry,
it is controlled by capitalists. If they "let themselves be seduced from their
pursuit of profits to the enchantments of art, they would be bankrupt
before they knew where they were. You cannot combine the pursuit of
money with the pursuit of art" ("The Drama, the Theatre, and the
Films," 1 September 1924). Although they are not so seduced, they
hire people who pursue art and, like most employers, aim to pay their
employees as little as necessary in return for as much as they can get.
Shaw guided himself accordingly, telling Samuel Goldwyn, who professed
to care only about art and not about money, that he and Goldwyn were
incompatible because "I'm only a tradesman and care only about money"
("Shaw in Film Debut," 9 October 1926). When Shaw dealt with busi-
nessmen, he was businesslike, doing all he could to protect his interests.
"All film adventurers denounce one another as crooks, mostly quite
justly," he said. However, if a producer gave him "the name and address
of any film producer who is not a crook (according to all the others) I
shall be obliged to him."[7] Although he made such statements without
rancor, he dealt with the crooks without illusions.

When talkies replaced silent movies, he perceived that an author's sale of national rights became more profitable than a sale of worldwide rights. An additional advantage was "in the case of a failure that the eggs are not all in one basket" ("[The Nationalization of Cinema]," 13 February 1935). In defiance of film corporations, he insisted on national rights or single-language rights when different countries shared the same language (Austria, Germany, and German-speaking Switzerland, for example), and these rights were not sales but licenses for five-year periods (see appendix). When a film satisfied him and when it was profitable, he renewed the license. He rejected lump-sum payments in favor of 10 percent of the gross paid by exhibitors to the manufacturer or to an intermediary between the exhibitor and manufacturer, unless the manufacturer were the distributor, in which case his royalty was 5 percent of the gross paid by the public at cinema houses. He levied percentages on the gross rather than on profits, since "[t]here may be no profit but there are always receipts and sometimes it may take ten lawsuits to determine what the profits are but you can always determine the receipts."[8] However, the last selection in this book shows that he used common sense. When his single-language rights policy conflicted with an Italian law that if an English-language movie were produced in Italy it must also be produced in Italian, he proposed two contracts, one for each language.

Cinema, he predicted very early, is "a much more momentous invention than printing was." It "tells its story to the illiterate as well as to the literate," whom it keeps "fascinated as if by a serpent's eye." For this reason, it will "produce effects that all the cheap books in the world could never produce." It will "form the mind of England. The national conscience, the national ideals and tests of conduct, will be those of the film" ("The Cinema as a Moral Leveler," 27 June 1914). Will its effects be benign or malign? "No art can have power for good without having power for evil also. If you teach a child to write, you thereby teach it to forge cheques as much as to write poems" ("What I Think of the Cinema," 13 March 1920).

Cinema's "colossal proportions make mediocrity compulsory," for movies are distributed in cosmopolitan cities and villages throughout the world, and they aim to please everyone ("The Drama, the Theatre, and the Films," 1 September 1924). In words that resonate today, when the millennium is imminent, Shaw describes the result of "leveling down" movies to the lowest common denominator of audiences:

> The melodramas are more platitudinous than melodrama has ever been before. The farces, more crudely knockabout than any harlequinade ever enacted by living performers, are redeemed only by the fantastic impossibilities which the trickery of the film makes practicable. There is no comedy, no wit, no criticism of morals by ridicule or otherwise, no exposure of the unpleasant consequences of romantic sentimentality and reckless tomfoolery in real life, nothing that could give a disagreeable shock to the stupid or shake the self-complacency of the smug. ("The Cinema as a Moral Leveler," 27 June 1914)

How would movies affect the theatre? Even in the early days of the silents, Shaw was aware that movie firms experimented with synchronized sound. "It looks as if we were within sight of a revolution in theatrical business," he prophesied, and if the figures on screen could talk, audiences would not pay to see performances by mediocre touring or repertory companies ("[A Theatrical Revolution]," 15 May 1912). When the figures did talk, he repeated, "People wont accept third rate actors when they can see and hear 'stars' on the screen" ("The Living Talkies," November 1929). Once filmmakers and actors mastered the technique of talking films, they would play the drama off the stage. As a consequence, "ninetynine per cent of the present occupation of the theatre will be gone; and the remaining one per cent will consist in training the public to appreciate the novelties of the cinematic pioneers" ("Relation of the Cinema to the Theatre," 9 May 1932). Two years earlier, he predicted, "[t]he theatre may survive as a place where people are taught to act, but apart from that there will be nothing but 'talkies' soon" ("Shaw Asserts Theatre Is Lost," 8 August 1930). True to his forecast, actors in the 1990s learn their art in the theatre, then move to and occasionally back from the cinema. In our time, theatre workers "are eager to view their work as R-&-D for the [Film] Industry," and to movie producers, as television and stage producer Joseph Stern states apropos both writing and acting, "'theatre is just another place to find material.'"[9]

One of the unique qualities of Shaw's predictions is that they are not lamentations for the death of a golden era. Before talkies, he forecast cultural enrichment, since when audiences "can see and hear Forbes-Robertson's Hamlet . . . well produced, it will be possible for our young people to grow up in healthy remoteness from the crowded masses and slums of big cities without also growing up as savages" ("What the Films May Do to the Drama," May 1915). Even in pre-talkie days, he said, "the cinema takes from the theatre only those plays that have no business there; and the resultant pressure on the theatres to find plays with some brains in them is of incalculable benefit to the drama" ("Plays with Brains," 28 October 1923). Cinema "will kill the theatres which are doing what the film does better, and bring to life the dying theatre which does what the film cannot do at all" ("What I Think of the Cinema," 13 March 1920). In addition to filming real rather than fake locales (forests and waterfalls, for instance), movies do better because "you can select all the perfect bits from your rehearsals (every rehearsal hits off some passage to perfection) and piece them together into a perfect performance," thereby reaching "a point of excellence unattainable by the stage" ("[The Value of Film Rights and of Editing]," 4 December 1928). When studios "can be persuaded that a good play is not ready to be photographed until the actors have grown into it as completely as they do in the theatre after not only a month's rehearsal but a month's performance before the public," then the quality of film versions of plays will improve enormously (*"Arms and the Man* on the Screen," [July] 1932). What Shaw says of plays onstage applies as well, as movie actors now recognize, to rehearsing original screenplays. Directors who understand how to work with actors and are not merely photographers also recognize this to be the case.

A problem facing filmmakers then and now, despite greater permissiveness today, is censorship. To Shaw, movie censorship perpetuates mediocrity and conventional morality while preventing intellectually serious work. Censorship gives the job of banning films that may be detrimental to public morals "to some frail and erring mortal man," whom it makes "omnipotent on the assumption that his official status will make him infallible and omniscient" ("Mr. G. B. Shaw on Film Censorship," 20 January 1935). Because he becomes neither, he compiles a list of forbidden words and subjects, "usually religion and sex," and through his regulations, "the pornographers can easily drive a coach and six, as it is useless to check up on the letter if the spirit still eludes. But the serious plays like Saint Joan get stopped because they take the censorships completely out of their depth" ("*Saint Joan* Banned," 14 September 1936). Sex "is a perfectly legitimate element in all the fine arts that deal directly with humanity," and "if a new public inquiry is set on foot people who consider sex as sinful in itself must be excluded from it like other lunatics" ("Mr. G. B. Shaw on Film Censorship," 20 January 1935). Censorship also derives from class warfare, thus the British ban (since lifted) on "[o]ne of the best films ever produced as a work of pictorial art," Eisenstein's *Potemkin*. "The screen may wallow in every extremity of vulgarity and villainy provided it whitewashes authority. But let it shew a single fleck on the whitewash, and no excellence, moral, pictorial, or histrionic, can save it from prompt suppression and defamation" ("Views of the Censorship," April–May 1928).

Shaw was wary of permitting his plays to be filmed. Early in the silent era, he concluded that when audiences see a movie version of a play, they do not go to the theatre when that play is revived. Soon, he recognized that after the run and tours of one of his plays, he might license a film version for five years, since a new major stage production would not occur for at least that long. Another reason he held out was high taxation in more than one country, a legitimate concern. However, the major reason for his refusals was that the screen was silent. Movies remove from a play the only feature that distinguishes *King Lear* from a tawdry melodrama—dialogue—and a film's success "is in direct proportion to the quantity" of visual matter interpolated by the director ("The Theatre and the Film," September 1921). To Shaw, "a play with the words left out is a play spoilt; and all those filmings of plays written to be spoken as well as seen are boresome blunders except when the dialogue is so worthless that it is a hindrance instead of a help" ("The Drama, the Theatre, and the Films," 1 September 1924).

What about subtitles? Take this speech: "I mean to. See? I never made up my mind to do a thing yet that I didn't bring it off. That's the sort of man I am." The lines seem to come from movieland, not from Shawville, yet they are from a speech by Mangan in act 1 of *Heartbreak House*, which Shaw completed in 1917 (I added apostrophes to *didnt* and *Thats* in order not to give away the source). The point is the dialogue that follows, which reflects Shaw's view of subtitles:

> CAPTAIN SHOTOVER. You frequent picture palaces.
> MANGAN. Perhaps I do. Who told you?
> CAPTAIN SHOTOVER. Talk like a man, not like a movy.[10]

Shotover's belief is consistent with Shaw's, for example, "The magnates might pay for literate subtitles; but one of the joys of the cinema would be gone without such gems as 'Christian: Allah didst make thee wondrous strong and fair'" ("The Drama, the Theatre, and the Films," 1 September 1924), in other words, those of the opening of this paragraph, "What *about* subtitles!"

In Shaw's words, "the silent film was no use to me. . . . When movies became talkies my turn came" ("A Question Too Many," 12 September 1936). Film magnates made new offers. "But when we came down to the tacks, I found that the film corporations were nearly as far as ever from real play screening. The only business they had mastered was the Movie business; and their notion of a screened play was really only a Movie with spoken subtitles" ("My First Talkie," [August] 1931). In 1952, MGM agreed. In *Singin' in the Rain*, a parody of Hollywood during the transition from silent to sound movies, a studio head dismisses the objection that he should not make talkies because no one in his studio knows anything about a sound film: "What do you have to know? It's a picture. You do what you always did. You just add talking to it." So they did, prompting Shaw's quip that most studios "still think that a play is only a movie with spoken subtitles" ("Witty Shaw 'Holds Court,'" 27 March 1933).

Shaw understood, as most film critics, producers, and directors of his time did not, the revolution created by the sound film. "Now that you have got the talkie and can have real drama you must not cling to . . . the old diorama," he maintained. To think that once you have talk you are in danger of losing movement is nonsense, for movement "is not the purpose or point of the drama" ("The Art of Talking for the Talkies," November 1936). When the cinema presents plays, "its function is the function of the theatre" ("Relation of the Cinema to the Theatre," 9 May 1932), and the idea "that there is any difference between the art of the playwright and that of the filmwright is a superstition from the days when the screen was dumb and the cinema was 'the pictures,' not the drama" ("*Cæsar and Cleopatra*," February 1945). Both "have to tell a story and make its characters live and seize and hold and guide the attention exactly as Shakespear or Molière did" ("Films, Plays, and G. B. Shaw," 1937). Nowadays, critics and practitioners echo Shaw. While mechanically reproduced drama differs from stage drama "in some of its techniques," says Martin Esslin, who has directed drama for BBC radio and for the stage, and who has written on both as well as on cinema and television, it "is also fundamentally drama and obeys the same basic principles of the psychology of perception and understanding from which all the techniques of dramatic communication derive."[11]

Today, Shaw's views are becoming truisms. For most readers of this book, who like its editor were born after 1927 when *The Jazz Singer*, the first generally acknowledged talkie, opened, sound movies have been part of the world longer than they have. Nowadays, talkies are more a part of most people's lives than living theatre. To millions, Shakespeare is the author of plays assigned in school and of movies directed by such people as Laurence Olivier, Franco Zeffirelli, and Kenneth Branagh. Typical of their conditioning to dramatic experience is the question a fifteen-year-old asked his teacher before the class attended a production at the National Theatre, whether Granville Barker's *The Madras House* would be in color.[12] Today's audiences regard the venue of a dramatic representation as largely immaterial. So did Shaw.

Still controversial today is the issue of language in cinema. To film theorists and moviemakers who grew up in the silent era or were influenced by those who did, language is primary to the theatre but an appendage to the screen, where nonverbal imagery is paramount. To Shaw, dialogue is a vital part of the higher drama of both. He believed that the distinction between language and nonverbal imagery in cinema is, in the terms of Samuel Johnson's statement that serves as epigraph to this introduction, custom rather than nature. The verbal and the visual are not mutually exclusive.

In Shaw's day overwhelmingly, and in our day largely, the typical view of moviemakers and critics is that dramatic dialogue in general and Shaw's in particular is, to cite cinema critic Robert C. Roman, "unsuited to the screen." To make it suited requires an adapter, who must invent action, which is minimal in Shaw's plays, and, as Roman puts it, must construct visual and verbal bridges "to connect action and other scenes in the film." Shaw's forte, of course, was writing dialogue for situations that were essentially intellectual; and all of his plays deal with *ideas*, which is the cause of the primary difficulty those who try to film Shaw must overcome."[13] Such a view begs the question: if such change is necessary, why bother to film the play? Shaw decried these notions of dialogue and bridges: "I dont believe that links and bridges are needed to connect the acts for filming. The audience will make the jump exactly as they do in the theatre" ("[New Scenes for the *Major Barbara* Film]," 21 November 1939). While he did not use the term *jump cut,* a technique not favored in his day, his statement is compatible with the device, which is favored in our day.

Common sense would dictate that if one undertakes to film a play by Shaw or anyone else, the director should make the most, not the least, of the play's assets, including language. The director would employ varying camera shots and angles (numerous or few), editing (much or little), tracking shots or panning shots, and reaction shots to enhance dialogue even if it were spoken in a single set. Essentially, this is Shaw's view. He chastised whoever would mutilate his language to make time for frequent changes of locale. Consider this statement:

> There is an enormous amount of nonsense talked about what is or is not "cinematic," and when a film is an adaptation of a play, there are some who jump to the conclusion that it cannot be true "cinema," that it must be "just a photographed play" . . . unless the scenes in the play are given visual movement which extends beyond the limits imposed by the stage set. Such people believe that if you have a scene in a play where two people are sitting talking to each other, the only escape from the theatrical medium is to start the dialogue in the room, get them to move out, dissolve to them on top of a bus, dissolve to them on . . . the Underground and finish them in a punt on the river. By doing this they believe they have translated a theatrical scene into film terms by giving it the kind of movement which is impossible in the theatre.
>
> This, of course, is a complete misunderstanding, both of the nature of dramatic movement and the fundamental difference between the theatre and the cinema. It is true that sometimes such movement is appropriate . . . but more often, the dramatic movement is in the growing tension between the two characters and depends on the ebb and flow of the dialogue. If you impose visual movement which neither accompanies the dialogue nor adds point to it by its very incongruity, especially movement which involves dissolving from one setting to another, you will find you have slowed down the real movement of the scene if not destroyed it altogether. It is perfectly possible to film a scenario out of a play without altering one comma, or adding one movement, and yet have achieved the necessary translation from one medium to another.

The author of these words is not Shaw but Anthony Asquith, who directed film versions of Shaw's *Pygmalion* and *The Doctor's Dilemma,*

Rattigan's *The Winslow Boy* and *The Browning Version*, and Wilde's *The Importance of Being Earnest*. "The heart of a Shaw scene," notes Asquith, "is nearly always a verbal one. . . . It is almost impossible to break up such scenes into small sections without destroying the general rhythm and also making it far harder for the actors." He tries "to make the visual flow and emphasis correspond to the rhythm and sense of the dialogue." [14] Whereas people like Roman focus on compensating for language in a talking film, those like Asquith focus on making the most of it. As with Shaw, the latter distinguish between nature and custom and recognize that dramatic dialogue and cinema are not mutually exclusive.

From the start, Shaw fathomed that film firms wanted from dramatists like him and Pinero not their distinctive dramatic writing but "simply our names on their bills" ("[The Writer and the Film Industry]," 12 December 1908). When asked why he rejected proposals to film his plays, he responded, "I have refused offers for the use of my name to attract audiences to demonstrations of how some crude and nameless author thinks my plays ought to have been written: but that is not the same thing" ("Films, Plays, and G. B. Shaw," 1937). That such practices were common is testified by a 1921 parody of a Hollywood announcement of a Shavian movie adaptation, which first trumpets the star's name in large capital letters, "TOOTSIE MINERVA in the Screen Classic Beautiful *A Woman's Embrace*," and follows with a credit in very small type and in parentheses, "Based on Bernard Shaw's famous drama of piety and passion, *Arms and the Man*," a title with less sex appeal than the movie's title, which is a more sexually explicit variation of it. The notice uses larger type and capital letters for a more important credit than the original dramatist: "A ROLLO B. SLUDGESMITH SUPER-PRODUCTION," after which comes a credit on a par with Shaw's: "Titles by Clinton H. Goldsmith." Among the film's changes, the Swiss captain becomes an American naval lieutenant, Raina a princess and "the passion lily of the rugged Balkans," and the Byronic Sergius "Karl von Donner, the notorious German spy, disguised as a Balkan officer." [15]

A Hollywood writer's adaptation of *The Devil's Disciple*, which made

Shaw cancel a proposed movie, and the German and Dutch film versions of *Pygmalion*, which he detested, support his apprehensions. Until Gabriel Pascal "descended on me out of the clouds," he said, "I could find nobody who wanted to do anything with my plays on the screen but mutilate them, murder them, give their cadavers to the nearest scrivener without a notion of how to tell the simplest story in dramatic action and instructed that there must be a new picture every ten seconds" ("[On Gabriel Pascal]," 19 September 1941). Is Hollywood's view of playwrights different today? As stage and screen producer Frederick Zollo states, screenwriters in Los Angeles are "'a notch below caterers,'" and as critic Robert Coe observes, "L.A. is still the place where a Pulitzer-winning playwright can take a meeting and be told, 'We love your play, Ms. Wasserstein, we just have trouble with the main character, the second act and the ending.'"[16] In our day as in Shaw's day, "Get me rewrite!" is the rule, not the exception.

When Shaw became involved in movie writing, his views of adaptation changed. In February 1915, he announced that *Great Catherine*, first published in English that month, "ought to do excellently on the movies. It is a scenario almost as it stands."[17] In 1929, he saw "no reason why *The Apple Cart*," which opened in London two months earlier, "should not be produced exactly as it stands" ("The Living Talkies," November 1929). When British International Pictures filmed *How He Lied to Her Husband* (1931), he did not alter the stage play; but in 1932, when it filmed *Arms and the Man*, he told the director of both that if he had time he "would half rewrite the play and invent at least fifty more changes of scene," but instead he advised—approving, disapproving, and suggesting cuts, new dialogue, and new scenes.[18] By 1938, a month before Pascal's British *Pygmalion* film went into production, he agreed that "a screen version of one of my plays may need new lines. But why should the bus driver or the bellhop write those lines? The obvious person is the author of the play: myself" ("Bernard Shaw Discusses the Cinema," 12 February 1938). He composed them and also new scenes. For *Major Barbara*, not only did he add scenes and cut dialogue, he offered Pascal a choice between cutting an entrance without subsequently explaining the character's presence or restoring eighteen deleted speeches; and he recommended the former because the latter "is much more stagey than screeny" ("[Revising *Major Barbara*]," 25 September 1940). After *Major Barbara* opened, he proclaimed, "All plays that are any good will have to be adapted to the screen" ("G. B. S. Tells," 9 November 1941). Although he urged directors not to treat his printed texts "with blindly superstitious reverence," he cautioned that they "must always be adapted intelligently to the studio, the screen, the stage, or whatever the physical conditions of performance may be" ("[The Need for Adaptation]," 3 October 1946). He objected not to rewrites but to who would do them. "Get me rewrite!" implies one who is not the original author. To Shaw, the author is the most qualified person for the job.

His view of the function of the director did not change. In the early days of cinema, he perceived that authors who do not direct their screenplays "will be at a huge disadvantage," for the director "will have the biggest pull in this business" ("[A Theatrical Revolution]," 15 May 1912). In movies as in the theatre, he believed, the director should serve the writer: "The playwright has to tell a good story, and the director to 'get it across'" ("Rules for Directors," July 1949). Despite his willingness to change his dialogue, he insisted on the primacy of the author. Nowadays, as in previous days, the senior partner in cinematic collaboration—as, for that matter, in theatrical collaboration—is whoever is most influential: usually a director, star, or producer. This practice, custom rather than nature, exists despite the fact that the superiority of, say, Hitchcock's *North by Northwest* to *Topaz*, Welles's *Citizen Kane* to *The Stranger*, Peckinpah's *The Wild Bunch* to *The Killer Elite*, and De Palma's *The Phantom of the Paradise* to *Raising Cain* is due not to the direction, since the latter of each pair is directed as well as the former, but to the screenplays (on some of which the director collaborated).

One critic today goes further than Shaw did: "[I]n the theatre, the writer is king and directors know their place, and that's the way it should be. Hollywood got this backward because film evolved from scriptless spectacle to silent film to talkie. By the time it became a fully literary activity, the director already had hegemony." This state of affairs, he concludes, has become worse, and "Hollywood's necessary-evil feeling about writers has gotten out of control."[19]

In cinema as in many other areas, Bernard Shaw was ahead of his time. The pages that follow reveal the wit and incisiveness he brings to this subject.

Notes

1. Reprinted in *Shaw's Music*, ed. Dan H. Laurence (London: Max Reinhardt, 1981), 2: 309.

2. Ivor Montagu, "Old Man's Mumble: Reflections on a Semi-Century," *Sight and Sound* 44 (Autumn 1975): 223.

3. London School of Economics and Political Science, Shaw Material, Parcel 26.

4. Quotations from Shaw's written and oral statements in this collection are identified parenthetically in the text.

5. Postcard to Percy Burton, 11 August 1913, published in *Boston Transcript* (?), ca. 1914, clipping in R. Lock scrapbook, New York Public Library (Courtesy of Dan H. Laurence).

6. London School of Economics, Shaw Material, Parcel 13.

7. Letters of 30 December 1935 and 16 January 1936, in *Bernard Shaw's Letters to Siegfried Trebitsch*, ed. Samuel A. Weiss (Stanford: Stanford University Press, 1986), 353–54.

8. Letter, addressee, and date not given, quoted in S. N. Behrman, *The Suspended Drawing-Room* (New York: Stein & Day, 1965), 77.

9. Robert Coe, "Let's Make a Deal," *American Theatre* 11 (July–August 1994): 18.

10. *The Bodley Head Bernard Shaw: Collected Plays with Their Prefaces*, ed. Dan H. Lawrence (London: Max Reinhardt, 1972), 5: 13. This passage is identical to that of the typescript, with holograph revisions, based on Shaw's shorthand original. See Bernard Shaw, *Heartbreak House: A Facsimile of the Revised Typescript* (New York: Garland Publishing, 1981), 46.

11. Martin Esslin, *An Anatomy of Drama* (London: Temple Smith, 1976), 12.

12. *Peter Hall's Diaries*, ed. John Goodwin (London: Hamish Hamilton, 1983), 339.

13. Robert C. Roman, "G. B. S. on the Screen," *Films in Review* 11 (August–September 1960): 406.

14. Anthony Asquith, "The Play's the Thing," *Films and Filming* 5 (February 1959): 13.

15. Robert A. Simon, "Shaw and Super-Shaw," *New York Post*, 2 January 1921 (clipping, Files of Dan H. Laurence).

16. Robert Coe, 16–17. Wendy Wasserstein's play is *The Heidi Chronicles*.

17. Letter to Miss Galbraith Welch, 23 February 1915, quoted in *Americana, Maps, Prints, Literature & Fine Books* (catalog of Sotheby Parke Bernet, Inc., New York, for auction sale 30 April 1975), no. 321.

18. Letter to Cecil Lewis, 17 April 1932, quoted in headnote, Bernard Shaw, *Collected Letters*, ed. Dan H. Laurence (London: Max Reinhardt, 1988), 4: 286.

19. John H. Richardson, "Dumb and Dumber," *New Republic* 212 (10 April 1995): 26–27.

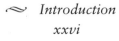

A Note on the Texts

OF THE one hundred seven separate items in this volume, including
the appendix, fifty-nine—more than half—will be new to today's readers.
Twelve are previously unpublished, one is published in full for the first
time, and forty-six appear in a collection of Shaw's writings for the first
time since their initial publication in newspapers or magazines. Abbreviations of this and other publishing information, as well as their sources
and the publishing history of selections previously published, appear
below the title of each item. For the explanation of these signs, see Sym-
bols and Abbreviations. Except for the appendix, the items are arranged
chronologically.

This book will be read and consulted by scholars, teachers, and students of cinema, drama, theatre, and Shaw studies; by directors and
actors; as well as by intelligent readers who are not specialists or practitioners but are interested in a good read. At least I hope so. In any case,
I have for this reason tried to follow a narrow line to determine those
references that require annotations, which are placed at the end of each
item, and those that do not. For example, although I assume that this
book's readers will not need annotations for Charlie Chaplin, Henrik
Ibsen, Friedrich Nietzsche, Eugene O'Neill, Ginger Rogers, and Oscar
Wilde, I believe that some readers will require notes for James M. Barrie,
Henri Bergson, Eugène Brieux, and Edmond Rostand. Whereas those
knowledgeable in cinema will find notes on Jesse Lasky, Max Linder, and
Norma Shearer, for instance, to be superfluous, those acquainted with
drama and theatre may need them; they are therefore annotated. Drama
and theatre historians will want no note for Granville Barker, Henry Irving, and Harry Lauder, but cinema experts may; they too are therefore
annotated.

Editorial interpolations are indicated by brackets. For the most part, I have, where necessary, altered the text to conform to Shaw's idiosyncratic spelling and punctuation. For example, he spells *Shakespeare* and *Chekhov* as *Shakespear* and *Tchekov*; he retains the old spelling *shew* (as in *sew*) rather than the newer *show*; he uses the American *labor* and *organize* rather than the British *labour* and *organise*; and he spells the noun *licence* but the verb *license*. Because he considers apostrophes unnecessary, he removes them to form such words as *dont*, *doesnt*, and *Ive*; but he retains them for such contractions as *I'll* and *I'm*. Despite the resemblance of his unapostrophed verb *cant* for the noun spelled the same way, I have followed his insistence on removing the apostrophe, since he believes that readers are unlikely to mistake the verb for the noun; in one instance, I have removed the apostrophe from the title of a newspaper article ("Shaw Not a Film Snob, but Cant Be a Dumb Dramatist," a problem another editor solved by abbreviating the title to "Shaw Not a Film Snob"). I have also followed his practice of removing periods after such abbreviations as "Mr." Instead of italicizing words and phrases for emphasis, Shaw demanded that his printers use spaces between letters and words for emphasis, and I have accommodated him. In his letters, he underscores for emphasis; because italics are a printer's device for underscored words and phrases in a manuscript, I have followed his publishing practice for his correspondence, using spaces for emphasis. I have complied with his practice of dropping commas before and after interrupting phrases that break a quotation into two parts and of keeping or placing commas in a series (first, second, and third). Although Shaw does not italicize titles, a practice I have followed, I have not allowed a foolish consistency to become my hobgoblin and have italicized titles of plays in annotations and in titles of Shaw's writings. Nor have I permitted another Shavian practice to become a hobgoblin: dropping one of two consecutive letters, as in *forgetting* and *omitting*, when readers would understand the word without it. Since Shavianizing such words, I have discovered, suggests an editor who is either illiterate or does not proofread, I have ignored Shavian in favor of conventional spelling.

Symbols and Abbreviations

Publishing Information

[ ]	Title between brackets is the editor's
C	Published in a collection of Shaw's writings for the first time
F	Published in full for the first time
P	Published for the first time
X	Extract

Types of Writing

HC	Holograph postal card
HL	Holograph letter
QI	Questionnaire-Interview
S	Symposium
SDI	Self-Drafted interview
SH	Shorthand draft or copy
TL	Typed letter
VR	Verbatim report of speech

Sources

AG	Bernard Shaw, *Agitations: Letters to the Press 1875–1958*, ed. Dan H. Laurence and James Rambeau (New York: Frederick Ungar, 1985).
BL	British Library, followed by additional manuscript number

BUL	Brown University Library, Sidney P. Albert Collection
CL	Bernard Shaw, *Collected Letters*, ed. Dan H. Laurence (London: Max Reinhardt) followed by volume number 3 (1985) or 4 (1988).
CPP	*The Bodley Head Bernard Shaw: Collected Plays with Their Prefaces*, ed. Dan H. Laurence (London: Max Reinhardt), followed by volume number 4 (1972) or 6 (1973).
Del	Files of Valerie Pascal Delacorte
DHL	Files of Dan H. Laurence
FL	Fales Library, New York University
HRHRC	Harry Ransom Humanities Research Center, University of Texas at Austin
IR	*Interviews and Recollections*, ed. A. M. Gibbs (Iowa City: University of Iowa Press, 1990).
PP	Bernard Shaw, *Platform and Pulpit*, ed. Dan H. Laurence (New York: Hill & Wang, 1961).
SC	*Bernard Shaw and Mrs. Patrick Campbell: Their Correspondence*, ed. Alan Dent (New York: Alfred A. Knopf, 1952).
SP	*Bernard Shaw and Gabriel Pascal*, ed. Bernard F. Dukore (Toronto: University of Toronto Press, 1996).
ST	*Shaw on Theatre*, ed. E. J. West (New York: Hill & Wang, 1958).
TDO	*The Drama Observed*, ed. Bernard F. Dukore (University Park: Pennsylvania State University Press, 1993).

Bernard Shaw on Cinema

[The Writer and the Film Industry]

(P/TL to Arthur W. Pinero, 12 December 1908/HRHRC)[1]

My dear Pinero,

This Strakosch communication is rather a floorer.[2] The first shock of these things always makes me feel the thinness of my favorite assumption of the capable man of affairs.

First, as to money, the bait held out is an alleged average chance of £120 for devising and presumably rehearsing a short but intense play with all the qualifications of a good ballet d'action. It is suggested that we might make nine hundred a year by inventing six of these; and I rather think it is implied that the job is rendered especially easy by the fact that we need not provide thoughtful or witty dialogue. Now, to you and me, this is very much as if they assured Paderewski that he would find it quite easy to give a particular sort of concert at which there would be no piano.[3] Take away our dialogue, and what better are we than ———— and ———— (I dare not fill in the names). Of course it seems quite possible that the synchronization of the gramophone and the cinematograph will presently get over this difficulty. I have myself seen one quite amusing little scene with dialogue; and Harry Lauder is almost improved by reproduction.[4] Still, for some time to come I doubt if it will be worth your while or mine (though the damned thing is such an irresistible toy that it fascinates the boy in me) to abandon the ordinary theatre for its sake, or even to throw off an occasional film in the intervals of the legitimate. However, if it does not pay or please us, other authors will find their account in it; and I suppose we must help to organize them. The main thing for the moment is that we should be careful how we enter into any contract until we find out what is going to be the real big concern in the business. This morning the Gramophone Company in the City[5] approached me again; and I have given them an appointment for next Saturday. But I do not want to make a contract with them only to find out afterwards that they are in a small way of business and are going to be either crushed or assimilated by some English Pathé. This cinematograph game is not, like the keeping of oilshops, a matter for a great number of small separate establishments: it is clearly a subject for organization on the biggest modern scale, by a bloated trust.[6] Therefore, the first thing to find out is who that trust is going to be; and until I have further information I do not see my way clearly. The Society of Authors should take it in hand, as far as it can be taken in hand, at once, so that we can discuss whether we can stand out for any better pecuniary terms and decide what conditions we should embody in a model agreement.

What they will want from me and from you is simply our names on their bills. I have no reasons to believe that I could devise anything for them more entertaining than the nameless authors of The Short-sighted Bicyclist, The Larcenous Bull-Dog, The Man Who Will Not Take No for an Answer (from the adored one's father), and so forth. When I look at these, I feel that I must either begin all over again or else resign myself to a job in the City for the rest of my life; but who knows? there may be a fresh career for both of us in this delirious field. But the Pathé people do not believe that: what they are calculating on is getting the people in by the attraction of our names, and then entertaining them with the Short-sighted Bicyclist, who is probably the invention of a foreman at forty-five francs a week.

Strakosch, you will notice, is only a promoter: he does not represent an existing organization; and when he says "I should not hesitate to come over at once and organize the affair with you," he implies that his notion is that you and the other authors should subscribe the capital and form a company. This implies, further, that Karl Strakosch must be either an exceptionally desperate adventurer or an exceptionally sanguinary fool; but although the thing will not be done in that way, yet it will be done. We shall come in simply as Rostand comes in with Pathé: that is, when the capital is found by capitalists and the business established by business men, then they will come to us for our names and services just as any theatrical management does.[7] All we have to consider is which management we shall deal with, and on what terms.

Of course I notice that on the second page of the communication Strakosch says "Our society is formed, our manufactories erected" etc.;

but what he means by this, God perhaps knows: I do not, for he adds "the firm of Pathé Brothers have allied themselves with us," and it is pretty evident that the firm of Pathé Bros have not united themselves with "all the writers, living or dead, dramatic authors and novelists," in any other sense than the one in which Drury Lane every year unites itself with Raleigh and Hamilton and Co. for the production of a melodrama![8] Strakosch, I think, must be one of those strange beings who drift into theatrical agency through a congenital incompetence for knowing or understanding anything whatever, and who suffer from chronic inflammation of the imagination set up the spectacle of large fortunes made by other people.

In short, dash me if I know what to say about it. As the translation you have sent me seems to be mimeographed, I take it that you have other copies, and that I may keep it unless I hear from you to the contrary.

     Yours ever,

     G. Bernard Shaw

1. A prolific, popular English dramatist, Pinero (next year, Sir Arthur Wing Pinero, 1855–1934) wrote farces and serious plays on social problems. As drama critic for the *Saturday Review* from 1895 to 1898, Shaw attacked the latter as mechanical contrivances that were conventional and that evaded real social problems. Here, Shaw wrote, from 10 Adelphi Terrace, London, as a colleague, not a critic.

2. Karl (sometimes spelled Carl) Strakosch (ca. 1859–1916), an impresario who lived and died in America, was the nephew of musical impresarios Max and Maurice Strakosch. He lived in Europe for some time, including the time of Shaw's letter.

3. Ignace Jan Paderewski (1860–1914) was a Polish pianist and composer.

4. The Scottish Harry Lauder (1870–1950), one of the most famous stars of the music-hall theatre, and the first to be knighted (in 1919), made his London début in 1900.

5. London's financial center; its American counterpart is Wall Street.

6. Oilshops were small general stores with an emphasis on domestic goods, such as oil for lamps and stoves.

7. Pathé Brothers was making a film version (released in 1909) of the play *Cyrano de Bergerac* (1897) by Edmond Rostand (1868–1918).

8. Cecil Raleigh (1856–1914) and Henry Hamilton (1853?–1918) were a popular British playwriting team.

[A Theatrical Revolution: Synchronized Movies and Records]

(X/HL to G. Herbert Thring, 15 May 1912/CL 3)[1]

Gaumont's new invention, by which he can make a talking record of eight minutes, is important.[2] It looks as if we were within sight of a revolution in theatrical business. I have haunted the electric theatres for some weeks past in the provinces; and everywhere the 30 [minute] film dramatic story is in the bills. Prices have risen to two shillings for the best seats; but in Blackpool you can have 15 hours of first class cinematography for sixpence. If only the figures could talk, nobody would ever look at a number two company again, much less a fit-up crowd.[3] Gaumont now says he can do the talking in 8 minute stretches, and hopes soon to do them in 40 minute stretches. We must get on to the subject of terms at once. Incidentally, authors who dont produce will be at a huge disadvantage; for the producer will have the biggest pull in this business. . . .[4]

. . . Meanwhile our members are left in ignorance of the one thing they want to know—how much to ask. We want to make them feel that they are getting something out of us—that in joining they have come out of darkness & confusion into light & certainty.

> In haste
> yrs ever
> G. Bernard Shaw

1. G(eorge) Herbert Thring (1859–1941) was secretary of the Society of Authors from 1892 to 1930. Shaw wrote the letter in Edstaston.

2. In 1901, Léon Ernest Gaumont (1864–1946), a French inventor and moviemaker, devised a way to synchronize a motion picture and a Gramophone.

3. A number two company tours a play while the original company continues to perform. A fit-up company is a touring troupe that uses a temporary stage and its equipment.

4. In British stage terminology of Shaw's day, the producer was what we call the director.

[Shaw's Fascination with Movies]

(X/HL (?) to Mrs. Patrick Campbell, 19 August 1912/SC)[1]

Do you ever study the cinema? I, who go to an ordinary theatre with effort and reluctance, cannot keep away from the cinema. The actor I know best is Max Linder, though I never heard his voice or saw his actual body in my life.[2] But the difficulty is that though good looks and grace are supremely important in the cinema, most of the films are still made from pictures of second, third, and fourth rate actresses, whose delighted willingness and energy, far from making up for their commonness, make it harder to bear. There is one woman whom I should shoot if her photograph were vulnerable. At Strassburg, however, I saw a drama which had evidently been played by a first rate Danish (or otherwise Scandinavian) company, with a really attractive leading lady, very sympathetic and expressive, without classical features but with sympathetic good looks, like Kate Rorke in the best days of her youth.[3] Here I saw a *femme fatale* who was a fine figure of a woman, but so hard that she wouldnt have been fatal to anything in my house except a black beetle if her foot happened on it. Also a *belle mère* [stepmother] who was a little more fascinating—so much so, indeed, that the audience applauded loudly when her husband, on looking out of the window and seeing her squeezing lemon juice into the medicine of her stepdaughter (to whom acid was fatal) seized a gun and shot her *sans phrase* [without saying a word]. It is something to have people care whether you are shot or not. But she was only £15 a week at the very outside. Now all these Dramas are dramas of Bella Donna in one version or another.[4] Twice I have seen a version called The Judgment of Solomon, which would have pleased me better if the bad mother hadnt been absurdly like Florence in her most maddening goodnatured aspect.[5] Besides, the baby, in spite of all the efforts of the performers to stifle it half the time and hide its cavernous mouth the other half, was evidently howling all through; so that Solomon would have been justified in having it cut in two merely to stop its noise.

Now I ask myself why should these mediocre ladies be preserved to all posterity whilst nothing remains of you but a few portraits which cannot reproduce your living charm. Nobody who has not seen you move—seen you "live and move and have your being"—has the faintest idea of your fascination.[6] I could make prettier photographs of women who, in action, are grimacing kangaroos. It would be well worth Pathé's while to pay you £5000 for a film, even if you make it a condition (which I should by no means advise you to do) that it was not to be exhibited in London. Think of that immortality—of beauty imperishable! Suppose you learnt that Mrs Siddons had had the opportunity of doing this, and hadnt done it through some snobbish scruple or other, wouldnt you swear at such little-minded folly?[7] Think of being a beautiful old lady with white hair, able at last to enter a room full of men without seeing them all coming on guard at once with the Almroth Wright terror of sex slavery in their souls, and yet able to see yourself at the height of your vigor and militant beauty![8] You say you want a job; why not this job, since Lubin is away and THE job must wait for him or some other Adonis capable of standing beside you without being ridiculous.[9]

> Your G. B. S.

1. Shaw had a long epistolary relationship with Mrs. Patrick Campbell (née Beatrice Stella Tanner, 1865–1940), a glamorous London stage star who in 1914 played Eliza Doolittle in the first English production of *Pygmalion*, which he directed. Shaw fell in love with her, but she rejected his amorous advances. He wrote this letter at the Hotel Excelsior, Nancy, France, where he was vacationing. There, he attended cinema houses, where he saw French and other European films, on which he comments.

2. Linder (né Gabriel-Maximilien Leuvielle, 1883–1925), an internationally popular silent film comedian, wrote and directed his own films.

3. Despite its small native market, Denmark was from 1909 to 1914 Europe's most thriving film center. In Berlin, London, New York, and Paris, its films vied with Hollywood's for popularity. Rorke (1866–1945), a popular London actress, played the title role of *Candida* in its first London production (1904).

4. Mrs. Patrick Campbell had a great success in the title role of this popular melodrama (1911) about an adventuress who tries to poison her husband by actor-playwright James Bernard Fagan (1873–1933), based on a best-selling novel (1909) by Robert Smythe Hichens (1864–1950).

5. Florence Farr (1860–1917), English actress with whom Shaw had a love affair, was an Ibsen pioneer. She played Blanche Sartorius and Louka in the first productions of *Widowers' Houses* and *Arms and the Man*.

6. The quotation is from Acts 17:28.

7. Sarah Siddons (1755–1831) was a great English tragic actress.

8. The medical discovery of Sir Colenso Ridgeon in *The Doctor's Dilemma* was based on that of Sir Almroth Wright (1861–1947), who was what today would be called sexist but what was then conventional.

9. In this cryptic reference to Mrs. Pat's Venus, Adonis may be Sigmund Lubin (1851–1923), executive director of the Lubin Film Manufacturing Co. of Philadelphia, Hollywood (from 1913), and for a time Germany.

Education and the Cinematograph

(C/*The Bioscope, Educational Supplement*, 18 June 1914)[1]

The cinematograph begins educating people when the projection lantern begins clicking, and does not stop until it leaves off. Whether it is shewing you what the South Polar ice barrier is like through the films of Mr Ponting, or making you silly and sentimental by pictorial novelets, it is educating you all the time.[2] And it is educating you far more effectively when you think it is only amusing you than when it is avowedly instructing you in the habits of lobsters.

It is impossible to say how the educational powers of the cinema can be "best" applied, because nobody knows what educational subject is most important; and in any case what is most important for Tom may be thrown away on Dick. Probably at present the best work the cinema does is the exhibition to masses of poor children of the habits, dress, manners, and surroundings of people who can afford to live decently.

An obvious application of the cinema to education is the reform of the Art School, with its "life class" studying an absurdly unlifelike naked human being in a condition of painful and hideous simulated petrification and paralysis. Our art students slave for years at this abomination, and finally deprive themselves of all power of drawing or even seeing a figure in action. The cinematograph can not only shew the figure in action, but can arrest the action at any instant, and thereby not only surprise here and there a moment at which the figure is graceful and expressive, but— what is more important—prove that ninetynine times out of a hundred the arrested action is artistically impossible, and that when the really successful draughtsman or sculptor presents a figure in action he combines several successive moments in his representation, and thus arrives at an outline no model can possibly give him.

In all athletic exercises, and in dancing, what is called "shewing form" can be done by the cinema. Much of the clumsiness and ugliness of our habits is simple ignorance; we have never seen anything better, and are even ashamed of pleasing our natural taste for something better, because it would make us look peculiar. The cinematograph, by familiarizing us with elegance, grace, beauty, and the rest of those immoral virtues which are so much more important than the moral ones, could easily make our ugliness look ridiculous. The moral virtues can take care of themselves only too well; it is our deficiency in the immoral ones that is keeping us back in the march of civilization.

1. The editors asked Shaw his views of the extent to which the cinema had educational possibilities and how it could best be applied to education.

2. Herbert G. Ponting (1870–1935), a British explorer who went to the South Pole with "Scott of the Antarctic" (Captain Robert Falcon Scott, 1868–1912) in 1912, made a documentary film, *Scott's Antarctic Expedition* (1913), in tinted color—one of the first major documentary films to record exploration.

The Cinema as a Moral Leveler

(*New Statesman*, 27 June 1914, *Special Supplement on the Modern Theatre/TDO*)

The cinema is a much more momentous invention than printing was. Before printing could affect you, you had to learn to read; and until 1870 you mostly had not learned to read. But even when you had, reading was not really a practical business for a manual laborer. Ask any man who has done eight or ten hours heavy manual labor what happens to him when he takes up a book. He will tell you that he falls asleep in less than two minutes. Now, the cinema tells its story to the illiterate as well as to the literate; and it keeps its victim (if you like to call him so) not only awake but fascinated as if by a serpent's eye. And that is why the cinema is going to produce effects that all the cheap books in the world could never produce.

The cinema is cheap. For a halfpenny a boy is allowed to enter and sit out three films. For a penny he can stay the whole way through the entertainment. Not, of course, at the fashionable West End cinemas, but in the poorer districts, where all cinemas fill up their vacant seats in this fashion. The penny is often very well spent indeed. Take the not uncommon case of a child whose mother is out at work until late in the evening. To keep him out of mischief whilst she is away, she can either lock him in or lock him out. Usually she locks him out, preferring that the risk of his doing mischief and stealing food should be borne by other people. To a boy so situated the hospitality of a warm picture theatre with an exciting entertainment is priceless; and the work of begging the necessary penny is an occupation whilst the condition of pennilessness lasts. The people who are agitating to have children excluded from these theatres (they have actually succeeded in some towns in Germany) should be executed without pity. As to the magistrates who bind boys over not to go to the cinema, an intelligent Home Secretary would ask them whether it had ever occurred to them to consider the alternatives open to the boy: loafing at the street corner, for instance. As it is—

Nevertheless these people are not wrong in regarding the question of the morality inculcated by the cinema as enormously important. The cinema is going to form the mind of England. The national conscience, the national ideals and tests of conduct, will be those of the film. And the way in which the question is being tackled is very characteristic of our public life. Certain people who have never been inside a picture palace are alarmed at the hideous immorality of the film plays, and are calling out for a censorship and for the exclusion of children under sixteen. Certain others, who, like myself, frequent the cinemas, testify to their desolating romantic morality, and ridicule the moral scare. And between the ignorant meddlesomeness of the one party and the laissez-faire of the other nothing sensible is likely to be done.

What neither of them sees is that the danger of the cinemas is not the danger of immorality, but of morality. The cinema must be not merely ordinarily and locally moral, but extraordinarily and internationally moral. A film must go round the world unchallenged if the maximum of profit is to be made from it. Ordinary theatres in London and Paris can specialize in pornographic farce because the relatively small class which tolerates and likes this sort of entertainment is numerous enough in huge cities to support one theatre. Such farces, if they go to the provinces, have to be bowdlerized either by omitting the objectionable passages or slurring them over. But a film cannot be bowdlerized: it must be as suitable for Clapham and Canterbury as for Leicester Square.[1]

The result may be studied at any picture palace. You have what an agricultural laborer thinks right and what an oldfashioned governess thinks properly sentimental. The melodramas are more platitudinous than melodrama has ever been before. The farces, more crudely knock-about than any harlequinade ever enacted by living performers, are redeemed only by the fantastic impossibilities which the trickery of the film makes practicable. There is no comedy, no wit, no criticism of morals by ridicule or otherwise, no exposure of the unpleasant consequences of romantic sentimentality and reckless tomfoolery in real life, nothing that could give a disagreeable shock to the stupid or shake the self-complacency of the smug. In the early days of the cinematograph, when it was a scarce and expensive curiosity, some of the films were clever and witty. All that is gone now. The leveling down has been thoroughly accomplished. The London boy is given the morality of the mining camp; and the Chinese pirate has to accept with reverence the proprieties of our cathedral towns.

Now leveling, though excellent in income, is disastrous in morals. The moment you allow one man to receive larger income than another you are on the road to ruin. But the moment you prevent one man having a more advanced morality than another you are on the same road. And here we are not concerned with the question of teaching the London boy the criticisms of current morality made by Nietzsche, Ibsen, and Strindberg, by Barker, Brieux, Galsworthy, Hankin, and self (pardon the popular phrase), nor the philosophy of Bergson.[2] These authors would not be popular with children in any case. But it is quite a mistake to suppose that conventional morality is all of one piece the world over. London cannot live on the morals of the Italian peasant or the Australian sheep farmer. What is more, high civilization is not compatible with the romance of the pioneer communities of Canada. Yet Commercialism forces such morals on the cinema.

The moral is, of course, that the State should endow the cinema, as it should endow all forms of art to the extent necessary to place its highest forms above the need for competition. The highest forms, like the lowest, are necessarily immoral because the morals of the community are simply its habits, good and bad; and the highest habits, like the lowest, are not attained to by enough people to make them general and therefore moral. Morality, in fact, is only popularity; and popular notions of virtuous conduct will no more keep a nation in the front rank of humanity than popular notions of science will keep it in the front rank of culture. Ragtimes are more moral than Beethoven's Symphonies; the Marriage of Kitty is more moral than any masterpiece of Euripides or Ibsen; Millais is more moral than Mantegna: that is why there is comparatively no money in Beethoven and Ibsen and Mantegna.[3] The London boy can hear a little Beethoven occasionally from an L.C.C. [London County Council] band, and may see Mantegna's work in the National Gallery. Ibsen is to be heard cheaply (in Yiddish) at the Pavilion Theatre in Whitechapel.

But the nameless exponents of worldwide vulgarity (vulgarity is another of the names of morality) have complete possession of the cinema.

Already there is a cry, if not a very loud one, for educational films, meaning, as far as my experience goes, something ending with a fight between an octopus and a lobster. I suggest that what is wanted is the endowment, either public or private, of a cinema theatre devoted wholly to the castigation by ridicule of current morality. Otherwise the next generation of Englishmen will no longer be English: they will represent a world average of character and conduct, which means that they will have rather less virtue than is needed to run Lapland. I shall be happy to contribute a few sample scenarios.

1. Shaw's observation that a film, to be successful, must befit a suburb, a cathedral town, and the center of London does not reckon with the bowdlerization that an editor's or censor's scissors make possible.

2. A dramatist, actor, director, and Shakespearean critic, Harley Granville Barker (1877–1946), who later hyphenated his name, had a close personal and professional relationship with Shaw. While his plays have been infrequently produced, some rank them among the best modern British dramas. As a director, he was a vital force in the English theatre in the early twentieth century; from 1904 to 1907 at the Court Theatre, he and J(ohn) E(ugene) Vedrenne (1867–1930) produced works the commercial theatre disdained, including the social dramas of the prolific, popular novelist John Galsworthy (1867–1933) and the satiric plays of Edward Charles St. John Hankin (1869–1909), both English. Their Shavian productions, directed by Shaw, established Shaw's playwriting reputation in England. Shaw championed the problem plays of Eugène Brieux (1858–1932), whom he considered the best French dramatist since Molière. The élan vital of the French philosopher Henri Bergson (1859–1941) resembles Shaw's Life Force, a phrase Shaw used first; and Bergson's work, such as *Creative Evolution* (1907), influenced Shaw.

3. *The Marriage of Kitty* (1902) by Cosmo Gordon Lennox (né Cosmo Stuart, 1869–1921) is a drama that, unlike the revivals of plays by Euripides, was a great commercial success. The painters Sir John Millais (1829–96), British, and Andrea Mantegna (b. 1431), Italian, stand in the same relationship as these dramatists.

What the Films May Do to the Drama

(QI/*Metropolitan Magazine* [New York], May 1915/TDO

A weekly paper devoted to the new and prodigious branch of human activity which is called the Motion Picture Industry lately approached me and, like the three highwaymen in the Pilgrim's Progress, or Wagner's Wotan in the smithy of Mime, propounded to me three questions. I thought I could answer them offhand in a few words; but when I tried to do it I found that the questions were not so simple as they were meant to be, and that my answers were expanding into little essays. I therefore took a little more pains with them than I had intended; and here is the result.

First Question: Is it advisable to invite the cooperation of skilled dramatists in the preparation and production of Film Drama?

Answer: It may be commercially advisable to engage highly skilled dramatists for film work because their reputations will draw audiences in a film theatre just as they will in an ordinary theatre. But it remains to be seen whether they possess any more of the special talent demanded by the film than film authors who could not produce even a tolerable charade in dialogue. Strike the dialogue out of Molière's Tartuffe, and what audience would bear its mere stage business? Imagine the scene in which Iago poisons Othello's mind against Desdemona conveyed by dumb show! What becomes of the difference between Shakespear and Sheridan Knowles on the film?[1] Or between Shakespear's Lear and anyone else's Lear? No; it seems to me that all the interest lies in the new opening for the mass of dramatic talent formerly disabled by incidental deficiencies of one sort or another that do not matter in the picture theatre. Take the actor or actress with bodily grace, facial expression, pantomimic genius, and ardent dramatic imagination, but with a wretched voice or a lisp or a stammer or a hopelessly foreign or socially unpresentable accent. Take again the would-be author who is full of plots and adventures and romances, but has no gift of verbal expression. These failures of the spoken drama may become the stars of the picture palace. And there are the authors with imagination, visualization, and first rate verbal gifts, who can write novels and epics, but cannot for the life of them write plays. Well, the film lends itself admirably to the succession of events proper to narrative and epic, but physically impracticable on the stage. Paradise Lost would make a far better film than Ibsen's John Gabriel Borkman, though Borkman is a dramatic masterpiece, and Milton could not write an effective play.

Thus the art of the theatre is a far more specialized, more limited, and consequently more exacting art than the art of the picture palace. In Europe and America there must be hundreds of talents available for the film to every one that is available for the stage; and it is in the enlistment of these talents rather than in the exploitation of established theatrical reputations that the special opportunity of the cinematograph lies.

Second Question: In what direction, in your opinion, should the development of the Film Drama be sought in order to raise the standard and insure the permanency of this new art?

Answer: The Film Drama must develop in every direction in which it gives honorable entertainment. The beauty of the picture is the aim which is, perhaps, least likely to take care of itself. There is room for improvement in the technical photography; and the comic films would be very much more amusing if they were acted quite seriously and not tomfooled with. Really accomplished producers, with a high artistic conscience, a keen sense of beauty, and what I call the tact of good fun, are more wanted than anything else at present.

Third Question: Do you think that when the standard of Film Drama has been so raised, it can ever successfully compete with the drama of the legitimate stage?

Answer: The picture theatre is bound to have—has already had, in fact—a most disturbing effect on the spoken drama. There exist an immense number of plays in which, though the plot is ingenious and exciting, the dialogue is worthless and superfluous, and in which material for half an hour's entertainment has been spun out into three acts or more. Of late years these plays have been compressed into their proper length of half an hour for use as sketches in Variety Theatres; but they can now be completely shorn of their dialogue and yet reexpanded into long film dramas, with scores of different scenes, by the representation of the narrated incidents (which take place off the stage in the original play) in the manner to which the film lends itself so effectively and easily. In this form such plays will be finally lost to the spoken drama, and the result will be that the theatre will find itself cut out by the picture palace as regards the very sort of play—the so-called "well-made" or "constructed" play of the French school—on which it has been for so long almost wholly dependent.[2]

Also, the elaborate art of scenic illusion will be hopelessly beaten and exposed by the pictures. The film can take you into the open air, over the hills and far away, up to the mountains and over the seas. It can shew you horses galloping down vistas of half a mile of road, or over moors and prairies, not to mention motor cars and aeroplanes and all sorts of conditions of life which the theatre can only imitate clumsily and distressingly when it dare attempt them at all. And the scene can be changed instantly: literally in the twinkling of an eye, sixty times in an hour. The illusion of theatrical scenery has always been itself an illusion: everyone who has rehearsed a play containing outdoor scenes knows how the first rehearsal with the scenery produces a disheartening and ridiculous disillusion, whereas the film, without sound or color or even orthochromatic color correction, transports the spectator to the very place that has been photographed. Against the competition of such powers of actual representation the theatre can do nothing except with indoor scenes, in which there is no deception; for what you see on the stage is what you see off it: the wall may be canvas instead of stone or brick, but its visible surface of paint or paper is the same as the visible surface of any real wall in any real room. What is more, most of the rooms represented in the picture palace are built up with stage scenery, and are no more "real rooms" than those in which the spoken drama is enacted.

Consequently the film will not put out of countenance the plays of Pinero, Ibsen, Brieux, Tchekov, and, in general, the serious plays of the last half century, because the limitations of the theatre forced these plays into sets of rooms which could be actually built on the stage and changed during the *entr'actes* [intervals or intermissions]. The intolerable stuffiness of these conditions has driven Barrie, Hauptmann, and myself to break loose into the open air: for example, in The Little Minister and Peter Pan, in The Sunken Bell and in Cæsar and Cleopatra, none of which can be presented in the theatre with anything approaching the realism of A Doll's House or The Second Mrs Tanqueray or the latest cowboy film drama from America.[3]

Now consider the fact that the drama at its highest points in the past—Greek tragedy and Elizabethan melodrama—made no use of deceptive scenery or costume. Even the comparatively childish medieval Scriptural theatre, though it delighted in toy hell mouths and gardens of Eden, and heavens and limbos and Mounts of Olive and high priests' houses, yet exhibited them all simultaneously side by side on the stage all through the performance, thereby disclaiming any pretence of deceiving the senses of the spectators, or doing anything more than play at these toys being the real things they represented, or rather symbolized. The Greek stage was an impressive tribune from which the tragedians declaimed, formed of a facade of pillars and entablatures which gave a lofty and solemn atmosphere to the tragedy, but in no way condescended to imitation of the natural features of the places in which the tragedy was supposed to occur. The Elizabethan stage was a platform built round a room or tent formed with curtains with a balcony above it. These remained unchanged throughout the performance. The actors, who were dressed in contemporary Elizabethan costumes, when they did not wear purely fantastic or conventional ones, spoke from the balcony when they were supposed to be speaking from a town wall or a window to the plain or street below; from the platform when they were supposed to be in the plain or street, and from the curtained room when they were supposed to be indoors. Mr William Poel has again and again given performances of Shakespear's plays under these conditions; and his performances have induced far more illusion than the elaborate stage pictures popularized by Charles Kean and continued by Irving, Augustin Daly, and Beerbohm Tree, with all the ruinous mutilations and delays they involve.[4] Finally Mr Granville-Barker has developed a new art of Shakespear and classical

production in which he uses the imposing columnar facade and entablatures of the Greek theatre, the platform or "apron" stage with different
suggestive levels of the Elizabethan playhouse, and the toy scenery of
the medieval stage (the fairies' hill in A Midsummer Night's Dream, for
example), with appropriately fantastic and beautiful costumes instead of
"costumes of the period": in short, he uses every device e x c e p t the
device of realistic historical "pretending" (it really cannot be called illusion) which was so incorrigible and ugly a habit of the XIX century
theatre.[5] By this revolution in dramatic representation he has not only
made it possible to present Shakespear's plays, or modern works like
Thomas Hardy's Dynasts, without omitting a line or interrupting the
rapid sequence of their action (an impossibility under the XIX century
conditions), but he has opened to dramatists a way of escape from the
eternal realistic modern interior and enabled them to indulge their imagination with a rapid succession of scenes in the open air, on the sea, in the
heavens above, in the earth beneath, and in the waters under the earth,
thereby relieving them of intolerable restrictions and of a frowsty,
unhealthy atmosphere, far more demoralizing to the theatre than its supposed natural tendency to licentiousness.[6]

The effect of the Film Drama on this development is very potent. By
accustoming the poorest playgoers to genuine realism in scenery at so low
a cost of representation and reproduction that our film companies can
afford to spend sums on the original production that would ruin the most
princely actor-manager, it reduces the would-be deceptive realistic scenery
of the spoken drama to absurdity, both artistically and economically, and
thereby gives a powerful and elevating impulse to the restoration of the
conditions under which the theatre attained its highest and freest point.

Consequently the answer to the third question is that Film Drama
will compete so successfully with the spoken drama that it will drive it
to its highest ground, and close all paths to it except those in which its
true glory lies: that is, the path of high human utterance of great thoughts
and great wit, of poesy and of prophecy. Or, as some of our more hopelessly prosaic critics call it, the path of Talk.

I am not forgetting the technical possibilities of the synchronized phonograph and cinematograph. I have heard a film sing, and wished it wouldnt; but that was the fault of the original singer and the imperfect synchronization. I have heard a film talk through a short scene quite amusingly and successfully. I have watched a long film drama and thanked heaven that the hero and heroine could not talk, for I knew only too well that they would bore me with sentimental twaddle, and that if they once began that, they would drive their audiences back into the circus, where the acrobats seldom disenchant us by opening their mouths. But I once saw an excellent film in which Sarah Bernhardt figures as Queen Elizabeth.[7] It was in a small town on the Welsh border, to which it could never have paid any manager to bring so expensive a star; and I realized that if the people there were ever to hear great plays handsomely mounted and spoken by famous actors (an absolutely necessary part of high popular culture), the synchronized cinema and gramophone was their only chance. Already they can hear the singers of Westminster Cathedral singing the masses of Palestrina; and only the other day the substitution of fibre for steel needles effected an amazing improvement in the reproduction of such music, the old snarl being softened and all but cured.[8] When they can see and hear Forbes-Robertson's Hamlet equally well produced, it will be possible for our young people to grow up in healthy remoteness from the crowded masses and slums of big cities without also growing up as savages.[9]

Also, by the way, Forbes-Robertson will not be condemned to the inhuman task of playing Hamlet for hundreds of consecutive nights, nor to relinquish his art as a painter under the strain of excessive and useless repetitions of his parts as an actor. What prodigious fee he will get for his filmed and recorded performance I dare not conjecture. At all events we shall hear no more of the fugitive fame of the actor's art which perishes with himself; for Robertson's Hamlet, filmed and recorded, may delight posterity when the name of the author is forgotten.

If this come to pass, the actor's fame will spread both in time and space. This is occurring already. I have never seen Max Linder in the flesh; nor have I even been within miles of the American Vitagraph company of players.[10] Yet I am as familiar with their persons and their acting as I was in my youth with Buckstone's Haymarket Company or later on with Augustin Daly's Company.[11] Had the scientific people been a generation earlier with their invention, all the young people could now see for themselves the enchanting young geniuses I still see when I meet Mrs Kendal and Ada Rehan.[12] And to think that they and Ellen Terry might have been creating a thousand new parts while they were repeating old ones in tedious long runs that only wasted their talents and staled their enthusiasm![13] And think, too, of the rehearsals in the open air instead of in a cold, sunless, theatre, with a T-piece to light the prompter.[14] Think of the gallops, the sousings in real rivers, the boatings on real salt waves, the flights in real aeroplanes they might have had had they not been in too great a hurry to come into the world! What a life it will be when all the theatres will be picture theatres, and all the plays immortal.

Think, too, of Democracy when all the great political speeches are filmed, and I shall be able to tell my audiences what I really think of them without having the platform stormed by an infuriated mob.

I shall not be at all surprised if the cinematograph and phonograph turn out to be the most revolutionary inventions since writing and printing, and, indeed, far more revolutionary than either; for the number of people who can read is small, the number of those who can read to any purpose much smaller, and the number of those who are too tired after a day's work to read without falling asleep enormous. But all except the blind and deaf can see and hear; and when they begin to see farther than their own noses and their own nurseries, people will begin to have some notion of the sort of world they are living in; and then we, too, shall see: what we shall see.

1. Like Shaw, an English dramatist born in Ireland, (James) Sheridan Knowles (1784–1862) wrote heroic tragedies in verse.

2. The well-made play (*pièce bien fait*) was an extremely popular type of drama constructed along the lines of a specific formula, whose foremost practitioners were (Augustin) Eugène Scribe (1791–1861) and Victorien Sardou (1831–1908), about whose artificially wrought plays Shaw coined the term *Sardoodledom*.

3. The plays of James (since 1913 Sir James) M(atthew) Barrie (1860–1937),

born in Scotland, include *The Little Minister* (1897, based on his 1891 novel) and *Peter Pan* (1905). *The Sunken Bell* (1896) is a verse drama by Germany's first important modern dramatist, Gerhart Hauptmann (1862–1946), who initially made his reputation as a naturalist. *The Second Mrs. Tanqueray* (1893) is by Pinero.

4. William Poel (1852–1954), English actor and director, pioneered uncut production of Shakespeare's plays under conditions as close as possible to those of the Elizabethan stage. His work was a reaction against the pictorially realistic scenery and mutilated Shakespearean texts used by such actor-managers as the English Charles Kean (1811–68), Sir Henry Irving (né John Henry Brodbribb, 1838–1905, the first actor to be knighted, in 1895), and Herbert (since 1907, Sir Herbert) Beerbohm Tree (1853–1917), who thirteen months before played Henry Higgins in the first English production of *Pygmalion*, and the American dramatist-manager Augustin Daly (1839–99).

5. The apron stage is so named because the apron is that part of the stage floor extending in front of the proscenium arch (or of the curtain).

6. *The Dynasts* is a drama in blank verse and prose (published in three volumes: 1904, 1906, 1908) by the English novelist Thomas Hardy (1840–1928).

7. *La reine Elisabeth* (1912).

8. The Italian composer of masses, Giovanni Pierluigi da Palestrina (1525–94), was director of music at St. Peter's Cathedral, Rome.

9. Johnston (since 1913, Sir Johnston) Forbes-Robertson (1853–1937), English actor-manager for whom Shaw wrote *Caesar and Cleopatra*.

10. Founded in 1896, the Vitagraph Company employed such future stars as Adolphe Menjou (1890–63) and Norma Talmadge (1897–1957); in 1925, Warner Brothers took over the company.

11. John Baldwin Buckstone (1802–79) was an English actor-manager-dramatist whose company performed at the Haymarket Theatre, London.

12. Mrs. Madge (later Dame Madge) Robertson Kendal (1848–1935) was an English actress. Ada Rehan (whose surname was a printer's error for Crehan, 1860–1916), American, was the leading lady in Augustin Daly's company.

13. Ellen (Alice) Terry (1847–1928), a major English actress, was Sir Henry Irving's leading lady; Shaw had a long epistolary relationship with her and wrote *Captain Brassbound's Conversion* for her.

14. A T-piece is a light bulb shaped like a tube.

Professional Association in Literature and the Fine Arts

(C/X/New Statesman, 28 April 1917)

In the theatre the sceneshifters are organized; and so are the bandsmen. But the Actors' Association is only a beginning, and is often hardly more than a name and an ideal. Actors have no common bond of class or standard of comfort or character. An actor may be a scholar and a gentleman, a knight or even an hereditary peer. He may also be an illiterate clown, sprung from the poorest class. An actress may marry into the aristocracy and be in every way worthy of her position, or she may be unpresentable in any but the most Bohemian circles. The illiterate and unpresentable may earn thirty shillings a week, or they may demand and obtain salaries which our greatest Shakespearean tragedians would never dream of. The modern invention of the cinematograph, which has opened lucrative careers to actors and actresses who could not speak a line presentably, has accentuated these discrepancies, which make fellowship impossible. As to economic organization, the highly paid stage favorite is eagerly offered better terms and more unreasonable privileges than any professional association could claim for its members; and the drudges are so poorly paid and so precariously situated that they dare not even seek protection of any sort, lest it should handicap them in obtaining engagements. The grievances of actors are unlimited hours of unpaid rehearsal, insanitary dressing rooms, and the competition of stagestruck amateurs who will not only act for nothing but actually pay for the privilege, either directly or in the form of financing the theatre on condition of playing the leading parts. In rank and file business, which requires no more professional skill than anyone can acquire with a little practice, actresses have to compete with women who use the stage only as an advertisement of their real profession, and who raise the standard of dress and depress the standard of remuneration until they drive genuine actresses from the stage. But the remedy seems to lie rather in legislation than in organization, which the circumstances make all but impossible.

Summing up the situation of the arts of self-expression, it appears that the most effective organizations in them are not strictly professional organizations at all, but organizations of teachers as such, or of proprietors of copyrights and performing rights as such. The teacher of thoroughbass finds that his place is with the teacher of thermodynamics and not with the violinist or composer; and the composer of a popular ragtime which rages on every gramophone must combine, not with the teacher of thoroughbass, but with the proprietor of a film which "features" Miss Mary Pickford or Mr Charles Chaplin. Thus the Society of Authors becomes the Society of Authors, Playwrights, and Composers, and has special committees of draughtsmen and composers, whilst the Royal Society of Literature, the Academic Committee, the Musical Association, the Art Workers' Guild, the Dramatists' Club, and the rest of the specifically professional organizations, insofar as they are not merely gossiping cliques, have to content themselves with discussing their art on its creative side, and indulging their impulses towards fellowship, whilst they cannot exercise any effective control of the social and political destinies of their professions. It is, of course, quite salutary and economical that the egotism and snobbery of professional sectionalism should be thus overridden by this need for coordination of the larger interests of the artists as members of the community with those of other pursuits; but unfortunately the alternative of not organizing at all is available, and is very largely adopted. The contrast between the extreme vehemence of individual opinion among artists and the ineffectiveness of their public opinion is striking. If they are not treated by statesmen as altogether negligible, it is rather from the benevolence their art inspires than from any respect for their powers of organizing and enforcing their interests on Parliament.

[Griffith's *Intolerance*]

(X/HL to Henry Neil, 14 May 1917/CL 3)[1]

I saw Intolerance. With the exception of the little uplift episode of the baby in the iron bed & the nurses dancing at the other end of the ward (which looked rather like an inspiration of H. N's) it was the most damnable entertainment and the wickedest waste of money within my experience. It was like turning over the leaves of a badly illustrated Bible (in monthly parts) for three hours that were like three years.

    GBS

1. Shaw wrote to Judge Henry Neil (H. N. in the letter) from his country home of Ayot St. Lawrence, Welwyn. Neil, a Chicagoan who advocated such social causes as pensions for mothers, was at this time associated with D. W. Griffith, director of *Intolerance* (1917).

[Filming Plays Fatal to Stage Productions]

(HC to Augustin Hamon, 20 April 1918/CL 3)[1]

You may tell all the Cinema people that none of my plays can be filmed. I have received many golden offers from Gaumont and the English and American firms; and at first I was disposed to accept them, and even began making a scenario of The Devil's Disciple.[2] Then Mrs Patrick Campbell, touring in America with Pygmalion and The Second Mrs Tanqueray, had to abandon Tanqueray because it had been filmed, and nobody would come to see it acted at theatre prices.[3] Another cheval de bataille [war horse] of hers, Bella Donna, was killed in London in the same way.[4] The film introduced a real river Nile, a real dahabeah, and a real hyena clawing at Bella Donna's grave in the desert. My first Pygmalion manager went bankrupt in America because one of his most expensive productions was met by a film which was advertised "Why pay 15f to see So & So when you can see it here for 30c!"[5] I made further enquiries, and the replies left no doubt that filming is fatal to a live play, though of course it cannot harm a dead one. So if I do anything for the cinema it will be an original scenario, and not an adaptation of one of my plays.

G. B. S.

1. Shaw wrote from 10 Adelphi Terrace to Augustin Hamon (1862–1945), a socialist-anarchist author and editor who, with his wife, Henriette (née Rynenbroeck), was his French translator since 1904.

2. In 1915, Shaw was negotiating for a film version of the play and wrote scenes for it, none of which has survived. In early 1939, he wrote new sequences for the opening of a talking film version, which are published in *The Collected Screenplays of Bernard Shaw*, ed. Bernard F. Dukore (Athens: University of Georgia Press, 1980).

3. *The Second Mrs. Tanqueray* was filmed in England in 1916.

4. A film version was made in America in 1915.

5. George C. Tyler (1867–1946), an important American manager, produced *Pygmalion*, which opened in New York on 12 October 1914 to enthusiastic reviews. Because of earlier financial problems, however, his firm, Liebler & Co., went bankrupt several weeks later.

[Shaw Refuses to License a Silent Film of *Pygmalion*]

(P/HL to William Lestocq, 19 February 1919/HRHRC)[1]

Pygmalion is not available for filming.

Never let anyone tempt you to have a play of yours filmed until it is stone dead. The picture palace kills it for the theatre with mortal certainty. Pygmalion is still alive and kicking very heartily.

Besides, how can you film "Not —— likely"?[2]

ever

G. Bernard Shaw

1. Shaw wrote to William Lestocq (1851?–1920), a successful English author of farcical comedy, from Ayot St. Lawrence.

2. The self-censored word is "bloody." Lestocq's response, if he responded, has not surfaced, but he might have replied, "Subtitles."

What I Think of the Cinema

(C/QI/*Picture Plays*, 13 March 1920)

Do you consider that kinema plays have an artistic value?

Yes.

Do you, as a dramatist, consider that the kinema is a serious rival to the theatre?

Yes and No. The kinema will kill the theatres which are doing what the film does better, and bring to life the dying theatre which does what the film cannot do at all.

Is film acting by members of the theatrical profession likely to influence, adversely or otherwise, the art as practised on the stage?

It is a godsend to them in every way.

What is your opinion of the average motion picture play?

The average motion picture play is not meant for me, so my opinion is not to the point.

Do you agree with those who hold that the kinema has a bad effect on young and impressionable minds?

It depends on the film and on the minds. No art can have power for good without having power for evil also. If you teach a child to write, you thereby teach it to forge cheques as much as to write poems.

[Filming a Work in the Public Domain]

(P/TL with a holograph postscript to Horace B. Liveright, 7 May 1920/FL)[1]

I am much obliged to you for your letter of the 21st April, and for the handsome offer it contains.

The situation is evidently not clear to these muddled men of business. To begin with, there is not the smallest reason, legally or morally, why they should not film Cashel Byron, or any other work that has fallen into the public domain, as innocently as they might film Hamlet or the Book of Genesis.[2] English film firms can film American non-copyright books; and if there is a grievance it is between the two nations, and not between individuals. I made Brentano's my publishers because they had been intelligent enough to "pirate" my books when nobody else thought them worth annexing. I have never put any difficulty in the way of filming Cashel Byron. To all offers I have made the same reply: "I have no rights to sell; and there is nothing for you to buy. I claim neither moral nor legal rights. Go ahead; and good luck to you."

Why is it that they dont go ahead? Simply because neither a publisher nor a manager will touch a book or a film that anyone can handle in competition with him if it turns out a big success. I speak from experience. There are certainly not less than a million words of my brightest writing which any American publisher can reprint tomorrow without asking my leave or paying me a farthing: but the very men to whom I have pointed this out have preferred to offer me a thousand dollars for my name at the end of an article w h i c h t h e y w o u l d g e t w r i t t e n f o r m e, because they could have that all to themselves. That is why Cashel Byron has been lying there derelict and untouched ever since the film business began, and why there is no such pressing danger of the claim being jumped as you think.

Your cousin had better get a legal opinion (for what it may be worth) as to whether, if I wrote a scenario of Cashel Byron and registered in Washington, and he filmed it, its copyright could be pleaded against any unauthorized film made subsequently, or at least whether the point would be doubtful enough to prevent any "pirate" from taking the risk. If counsel's opinion were favorable I should have no scruple in taking all I could get for the scenario: indeed the only doubt is whether I could get enough for it to make it worth my while to write it. I can get $750 as a journalist for writing a thousand words; and therefore I should probably open my mouth a little wider [for] $8000: say by taking it as an advance on royalties instead of a final payment.

However, the first thing for your cousin to settle is whether he or his lawyers can devise any means by which I can sell him a protection against competition if he films Cashel Byron. Failing that he had better go ahead freely with my assurance that I shall not bear the slightest malice, or else consider whether it is really worth his while to invest the cost of a film production at the risk of rival firms doing the same and dividing the market.

Let me add that as the book is out of copyright in several continental countries, and so-called piratical editions have appeared, the legal point arises as to whether the authors of these piratical translations have acquired any rights. But I should say that they have not unless their translations were actually used by the writer of the scenario.[3]

Faithfully,

G. Bernard Shaw

PS   I forgot to say that if I sell a film right, I must sell it in England to somebody in England. If I sold it to you, the price would be subject to United States taxation, State of New York taxation, and British taxation, which would amount to m o r e   t h a n 100 cents per dollar: that is, I should have to pay more than I should receive.

1. Liveright (1886–1933), to whom Shaw wrote from 10 Adelphi Terrace, was president of the American publishing firm Boni and Liveright, which was founded two years earlier.

2. *Cashel Byron's Profession*, Shaw's fourth novel, written in 1882, was first published in 1886.

3. The following year, *Cashel Byron's Profession* was filmed in Czechoslovakia under the title *Roman Boxera*. No competing movie was made then or later, anywhere.

G. B. S. Replies to Mr. Lasky

(C/*Daily Express*, 22 June 1920)[1]

Mr Lasky is, of course, quite right: the film is a magnificent opportunity for imaginative fiction.

He might have gone so far as to say that the screen is a better medium for popular romance than the printed page, especially with paper at its present price.

The only thing the screen cannot give is dialogue and the customary psychological expatiations on which the characters think and feel.

Now many—I had almost ventured to write most—novelists cannot write what a playwright would call dialogue at all; any actress can do better by making faces; and as to the psychological essays, they are only padding and unmitigated tosh at that.

But why does not Mr Lasky crush all opposition by simply coming to figures? Novelists with the few dazzling exceptions that everyone thinks about, are a needy and consequently intimidated folk.

Mr Lasky has nothing to do but say how much, at a moderate estimate, he can afford to pay an author in advance of royalties for a promising scenario, and how much a successful one might eventually bring in to its inventor, and he will get hundreds of scenarios from our novelists as soon as they can get them down on paper.

If the film companies would offer a quarter as much to any novelist for a scenario as they eagerly pay to an American producer to spoil it and spend £50,000 in the process, it would not be necessary to write letters to the papers asking novelists to come forward; rather would it be advisable to engage extra police to stem the rush.

Mr. Lasky offers us opportunities of propagating our gospel in all lands. Most of us have no gospel to propagate, and want new clothes very badly.

When Mr Lasky comes down to tin tacks we shall all be on his doorstep.

1. In "Is the Day of Novels Past?" *Daily Express*, 7 June 1920, Jesse L. Lasky (1880–1958), American, first vice-president of the Famous Players-Lasky Corporation, declared that cinema was supplanting novels and plays. Because of cinema's worldwide influence, he challenged, "the time has come when authors must choose whether they want to write for the screen or write for a few."

G. B. S. on Films Again

(C/*Daily Express*, 30 June 1920)[1]

Mr Lasky will do no good if he leaves it at that.

Let me ask him a question. Has he ever lost a valuable dog, and advertised that anyone returning it to his house will be suitably rewarded?

If he has, I venture to guess with absolute confidence that the dog was not returned to his house. What happened was that a humble sportsman called on him to say that he knew a man who was told by a policeman who had a sister, a barmaid, whose young man's mother's little niece thought she saw a dog that might be the dog in the area of a house that might be the house in Somerstown, and that he (the sportsman) might possibly be able to follow up this clue and recover the animal if he were empowered to offer a definite sum to the Somerstown householders.

The moral is obvious. It is no use announcing that the novelist who writes a good film scenario will be suitably rewarded. No sportsman will come along to make Mr Lasky name a figure. Novelists are shy birds when they are out of their own field.

They are accustomed to being taken advantage of by publishers and they believe that filmers are more ruthless than publishers. They perceive Mr Lasky's reluctance to name a minimum sum, and conclude that he is waiting to see how little they will take, or how much they will pay him for the honor and glory of appearing on the screen.

Now, surely, Mr Lasky might quite safely say that if a scenario is worth filming at all it is worth advancing a hundred pounds on to the author. As a matter of fact, it is worth much more; but a hundred pounds would do the trick with all the novelists who have not been already approached with larger offers, and taught that they can get ten times that amount.

Mr Lasky says that "responsible film companies are not given to paying American or any other producers to spoil a film any more than theatrical managers are given to paying producers to spoil a play." That is an admission, not a denial. Theatrical managers d o pay producers to spoil plays.

I am speaking, of course, of managers who are men of business and not artists. A man of business cannot, as such, judge whether a film or a play is a good one or not: he only knows what it costs him; and if a good producer gets an effect for five shillings which a bad one fails to get for five thousand pounds, the man of business concludes that the bad producer's work must be worth twenty thousand times as much as the good one's.

As a practical producer and author I can assure Mr Lasky that most films contain dead wood enough to build a fishing fleet, and that if authors would only learn the technical business of the screen and stage, which should be child's play to anyone with literary qualifications, they could save the film firms much more than they would cost them in author's fees at double what they would dream of asking at present.

1. On 24 June ("Mr. Lasky to G. B. S."), the *Daily Express* printed Lasky's reply to Shaw. Lasky called all financial transactions matters of individual, "private negotiation," which he offered to conduct with well-known authors. Since he opposed unions of writers or others, he would not set a minimum payment. "[P]rivate negotiation" is a euphemism for anti-minimum salary.

[Movie Rights, Taxes, and Options]

(TL to G. Herbert Thring, 4 February 1921/CL 3)

Welcome home.[1]

Hearst has sounded me on the subject of films; but he has never suggested that his very handsome purchases of serial rights from me should carry Movie Rights with them.[2] On the contrary, it is I who have been sounding him on the subject, because if I sell a film for £10,000 down, the taxation is so enormous, both on the sum itself and on all the rest of my income (which is raised in the scale by the addition of this big sum), that I prefer an annual payment spread over years; and yet as the film firms are here today and gone tomorrow, one cannot trust to anything but a lump sum in dealing with them. A permanent institution like W.R.H. would be much safer.

Hearst, like all men of business, will not pay for anything that he can get for nothing—why should he?—but when he must pay nobody pays like him. It is therefore up to the authors to take care of themselves. If they give him an option they should give it for a stated time, and make him pay for it. If they neglect that obvious precaution, they have themselves to thank.

I have made no Movie contract with him yet, nor with anyone else.

> ever
>
> G. Bernard Shaw

1. To London. Shaw wrote from 10 Adelphi Terrace.

2. The American newspaper magnate William Randolph Hearst (1863–1951) founded Cosmopolitan Pictures in 1919 to produce films starring his mistress Marion Davies (née Marion Cecilia Douras, 1897–1961). After 1923, Metro-Goldwyn-Mayer absorbed Cosmopolitan, and Davies acted for MGM.

[Taxation and Windfall Income from Films]

(X/TL to William Archer, 16 March 1921/CL 3)[1]

I hear that your play has been a big success in America. I do not know whether you have come back yet; but I take my chance of this reaching you in London.

Your fees and your film rights will bring you in a lot of money; but, unless you are careful, the United States Government, the State of New York, and the British Exchequer will strip you of half of it or more. You cannot escape both Income Taxes; but if you pay the American tax and immediately invest the balance there (not necessarily in American securities) so that it reaches this country in the form of capital you need not pay British income tax on it, nor on the proceeds of your subsequent sale of it if you sell it.

You need have no compunction in taking advantage of this privilege which the capitalists have reserved for themselves, because the taxation of author's royalties is taxation of capital in a very thin disguise; and by tearing the disguise off you obtain no advantage that is not already enjoyed by every financier.

Perhaps you know all this; but then again perhaps you dont. I did not know it myself until very recently. Hence this letter. . . .

Do not let your film rights go too cheap; and do not, as the silly American authors do, give the manager half.[2] I have been offered 20,000 pounds sterling (not dollars) per year for five years for two films of my old plays each year. That sort of insanity has gone bang now; but still it indicates how much money there is in the business.

        ever

        G. B. S.

1. Scottish critic, Ibsen translator, and dramatist, Archer (1856–1924) was one of Shaw's best friends from their meeting in the British Museum's Reading Room about 1883 until his death. Shaw wrote to him from 10 Adelphi Terrace.

2. Archer's melodrama *The Green Goddess* (1921) was an enormous hit on

the stage. It was made into silent and talking films (1923, 1930). In all three, the leading role was played by George Arliss (né George Augustus Andrews, 1868–1946), a popular star of stage, then of silent and talking films.

Would Shakespear Have Liked Charlie Chaplin?

(C/Bookman's Journal and Print Collector, 13 May 1921)

In my opinion the Governors of the Stratford Memorial Theatre have acted very sensibly in resolving to use the theatre for the art of the cinema instead of leaving it to eat its head off or harbor casual touring companies or strolling entertainers, very few of whom provide as edifying an entertainment as a well-conducted cinema theatre with a good orchestra. There is nothing wrong with the cinema that is not equally wrong with the theatre; and until Mr Bridges Adams brought genuine Shakespear performances to Stratford the so-called performances of Shakespear's plays there were a far grosser insult to his art, his authority, and his memory than the films of Mr Chaplin, in whom Shakespear would have delighted.[1]

1. In 1919, the director William Bridges-Adams (1889–1965) was appointed director of the Stratford-on-Avon Shakespeare Festival and founded the New Shakespeare Company, which became the Stratford-on-Avon Festival Company.

Cooperative Movies: Mr Shaw's Support of the Manchester Project

(C/Observer, 29 May 1921)

There is no reason why cinema theatres should not be added to the list of public wants provided for by the cooperative movement. They are quite unlike ordinary theatres, the management of which is a series of desperate gambles by infatuated plungers depending on 10 per cent of successes to wipe out 90 per cent of disastrous failures. It is almost inconceivable for a well conducted comfortable picture palace, with good music, not to pay its way in any populous place, even through the slumpiest slump; and at most times the profits ought to be so large and so easily earned that it is absurd that the public that provides them out of its earnings should not share them.

The dividend on a year's moviegoing by a workingclass family would help it very considerably, to say nothing of the improvement of its mind by the films. So obviously a step in cooperation is bound to come.

The Theatre and the Film

(*C/S/Referee*, 4 September 1921)

I agree with Brieux that cinematography is an art in itself, and that the practice of transferring stage plays from the stage to the screen is a superstition.[1] It imposes the very narrow physical limits of the stage on the practically boundless screen; and it deprives the stage play of the only feature that distinguishes Lear from Maria Marten or The Murder in the Red Barn; that is, the dialogue.[2] Its success is in direct proportion to the quantity of screen stuff interpolated by the film producer; the more complete the transformation, the better the result.

Authors should write for the stage and for the screen; but they should not try to kill the two birds with one stone.

1. In "The Future of the Film" (*Referee*, 28 August 1921), Eugène Brieux said that because plays adapted to the silent screen paid little attention to the conditions of this medium, films were "theatre without words," which retarded the advance of cinematic art. "The cinema should show us what the author, owing to the limitations of the stage, cannot show us," he added, and when a cinematic genius arrives, his major qualification will be that he never went to a theatre.

2. A popular melodrama (1830, anonymous), *Maria Marten* was sometimes called *The Red Barn*, the subtitle sometimes *The Red Barn Mystery*.

Authors' Rights: G. B. S. on Money and Art

(C/*Daily Telegraph*, 25 May 1922)[1]

In spite of all our campaign against publishers' agreements, the last few years have produced publishers' agreements which would have made the worst sharks of forty years ago blush. When you are dealing with people who are connected with theatres or films there is no definite standard of honesty. In their business, to keep them going at all, a series of ventures have got to be risked, and a great many of them will be failures. The thing is a continual gamble in which ten or twenty successes will have to pay for all that have gone before them, and the man who is doing that sort of business has got to make the best bargain he can. Do not go to lunch with a publisher or film person and think that because he is such a nice chap he wont "do" you. As a matter of fact, he will not "do" you; he is simply out to exact the most he can. It is not dishonest to get the best terms you can.

1. Partial VR of remarks at the annual meeting of the Society of Authors, Playwrights, and Composers. Paraphrases have been omitted.

Cinema or Pen?

(C/*Pall Mall Gazette*, 16 March 1923)

DOES THE CINEMA THREATEN THE PEN?
Why should it?
1. Scenarios have to be written, have they not?
2. If the scenario and the screen do in 5000 words what the novel does in 100,000 they save both the pen and the reader a great deal of trouble. If anyone "threatened" to save me trouble I should cry "Come on!"
3. There is practically unlimited work in the world waiting for the pen. Anything that sets the pen free from its present drudgeries sets it free, not

for idleness but for better employment. The introduction of calculating machines into business houses has saved oceans of ink and set many clerks free to do something better than adding as very slow and inefficient calculating machines; but nobody has made any fuss about that.

4. Fiction will take care of itself under any circumstances. Whether it is conveyed from the professional liar to his willing audience by handwriting, typewriting, cinematography, photophonography, telepathy, or what not, does not matter a rap to the art of fiction or its practitioners.

[Stage Theatres and Cinema Theatres]

(X/April 1923/*TDO*)[1]

I am in favor of making the playgoer comfortable. I admit that once you get him into the theatre he will endure anything, and that if you give him good drama and acting you give him, in effect, a chloroform that would make him forget St Lawrence's gridiron if he happened to be sitting on it.[2] But the difficulty is to get him in. If a good play makes him forget his discomfort, a bad one makes him remember it and fear it next time. He craves for the comfort of the cinema theatres, the best of which are made very comfortable because, as they are seldom full, nor ever expected to be full, and pay quite handsomely when they are what the manager of an ordinary theatre would call empty, the temptation to pack the seats together without regard to the comfort of the sitters is less strong than the desire to court their custom. Besides, the cinema relieves the spectator of all preoccupying and worrying self-consciousness—about his dress, for instance—whereas the ordinary theatre, the moment it takes its glaring lights off the actors, turns them full on to the blushing spectators. This factor in the success of the cinema is of enormous importance, but it is so little talked about that I should not be surprised if some idiot were to invent a means of making the screen visible in a fully lighted auditorium, and be hailed as a deliverer by the industry he was trying to ruin.

1. On 26 April 1923, Shaw sent this article to Lawrence Langner (1890–1962), codirector of the Theatre Guild, which produced so many Shavian plays in America that it was known as "The House of Shaw." The article was first published as "Wanted: A New Sort of Theatre" (*Theatre* [New York], May 1925) a month after *Caesar and Cleopatra* opened the organization's new Guild Theatre. This text collates those in the *Theatre* and Langner's *G. B. S. and the Lunatic* (New York: Atheneum, 1963).

2. While the Roman martyr Saint Lawrence was being roasted on a gridiron (ca. 258), he supposedly said to the judge, "*Assum est; versa et manduca!*" (It is well done; turn it over and eat it).

Plays with Brains: Mr. G. B. Shaw on Effect of Cinema Competition

(C/*Observer*, 28 October 1923)

When I began writing for the stage, I was met with continual complaints that my plays contained dialogue. The critics were not used to it; they cried "These are not plays, they are all talk." Our actors and actresses had nothing to say that mattered; they had to create the characters out of their own personality. They were wonderfully beautiful and fascinating, but they almost forgot how to speak; and some of them have not yet recovered the art.

The drama, though it still kept up a tedious convention of giving the performers certain clichés to learn and repeat, was really a speechless drama; and most of the critics of that day had lost the faculty of listening, and could only gloat over the spectacle. The cinema was a godsend to them; they loved Mary Pickford, not for her charm, but for the blessed certainty that she would never say anything, and that they could still earn their living without thinking. But the result was that the lovers of speechless drama deserted the theatre and crowded the cinemas. The theatres found themselves forced to find plays that had something to say instead of something to shew.

I can remember when the London stage had only two literary dramatists, helped out by one adapter. Now I can reel you off a dozen without stopping to think: and some of them are poets as well as playwrights. The cinema cannot oust them. It can, of course, take the skeletons of Macbeth, or Iris, or The Admirable Crichton, and make very entertaining films of them, with Shakespear, Pinero, and Barrie left out, and a good deal of photographed natural scenery bunged in; but these films are not substitutes for the plays; they are independent and quite different works, and will not lead to a single performance of Macbeth being dropped that would otherwise have been given.[1]

In short, the cinema takes from the theatre only those plays that have no business there; and the resultant pressure on the theatres to find plays with some brains in them is of incalculable benefit to the drama.

1. The 1916 *Macbeth*, starring Sir Herbert Beerbohm Tree; Cecil Hepworth's (1874–1953) 1915 movie of Pinero's *Iris* (1901); and Cecil B(lount) De Mille's version of *The Admirable Crichton* (1902), retitled *Male and Female* (1919).

The Drama, the Theatre, and the Films

(X/*Fortnightly Review*, 1 September 1924/TDO)[1]

HENDERSON: . . . And now we come to the films. Has the enormous development of the cinema industry benefited the drama, or the reverse?

SHAW: No; the colossal proportions make mediocrity compulsory. They aim at the average of an American millionaire and a Chinese coolie, a cathedral town governess and a mining village barmaid, because the film has to go everywhere and please everybody. They spread the drama enormously, but as they must interest a hundred percent of the population of the globe, barring infants in arms, they cannot afford to meddle with the upper ten percent theatre of the highbrows or the lower ten percent theatre of the blackguards. The result is that the movie play has supplanted the oldfashioned tract and Sunday School prize: it is reeking with morality, but dares not touch virtue. And virtue, which is defiant and contemptuous of morality, even when it has no practical quarrel with it, is the lifeblood of high drama.

HENDERSON: In spite of the fame of certain artistic directors—the Griffiths, De Milles, Lubitschs, and Dwans—perhaps it is true that the film industry is for the most part directed and controlled by people with imperfectly developed artistic instincts and ideals, who have their eyes fixed primarily on financial rewards.[2]

SHAW: All industries are brought under the control of such people by Capitalism. If the capitalists let themselves be seduced from their pursuit of profits to the enchantments of art, they would be bankrupt before they knew where they were. You cannot combine the pursuit of money with the pursuit of art.

HENDERSON: Would it not be better for film magnates to engage first rate authors to write directly for the films, paying them handsomely for their work, rather than paying enormous prices to an author of novel, story, or play, and then engaging a hack, at an absurdly low price, to prepare a scenario?

SHAW: Certainly not first rate authors: democracy prefers second best always. The magnates might pay for literate subtitles; but one of the joys of the cinema would be gone without such gems as "Christian: Allah didst make thee wondrous strong and fair." Seriously, though, the ignorance which leads to the employment of uneducated people to do professional work in modern industry is a scandal. It is just as bad in journalism. In my youth all writing was done by men who, if they had little Latin and less Greek, had at any rate been in schools where there was a pretence of teaching them; and they had all read the Bible, however reluctantly.[3] Nowadays that has all gone; literary work is entrusted to men and women so illiterate that the mystery is how they ever learnt the alphabet. They know next to nothing else, apparently. I agree with you as to the scenarios founded on existing plays and novels. Movie plays should be invented expressly for the screen by original imaginative visualizers. But you must remember that just as all our music consists of permutations and combinations of twelve notes, all our fiction consists of variations on a few plots; and it is in the words that the widest power of variation lies. Take that away and you will soon be so hard up for a new variation that you will snatch at anything—even at a Dickens plot—to enable you to carry on.

HENDERSON: . . . Have you in mind any definite suggestions for the further artistic development of films?

SHAW (*explosively*): Write better films, if you can: there is no other way. Development must come from the centre, not from the periphery. The limits of external encouragement have been reached long ago. Take a highbrow play to a Little Theatre, and ask the management to spend two or three thousand dollars on the production, and they will tell you that they cannot afford it.[4] Take an opium eater's dream to Los Angeles, and they will realize it for you; the more it costs the more they will believe in it. You can have a real Polar expedition, a real volcano, a reconstruction of the Roman Forum on the spot: anything you please, provided it is enormously costly. Wasted money, mostly. If the United States Government put a limit of $25,000 to the expenditure on any single noneducational film, the result would probably be an enormous improvement in the interest of the film drama, because film magnates would be forced to rely on dramatic imagination instead of on mere spectacle. Oh, those scenes of Oriental voluptuousness as imagined by a whaler's cabin boy! They would make a monk of Don Juan. Can you do nothing to stop them?

HENDERSON: . . . The [international] triumph, almost the monopoly, of the American film is uncontested. But are American films superior to all others?

SHAW (*decisively*): No. Many of them are full of the stupidest errors of judgment. Overdone and foolishly repeated strokes of expression; hideous make-ups; close-ups that an angel's face would not bear; hundreds of thousands of dollars spent on spoiling effects that I or any competent producer could secure quickly and certainly at a cost of ten cents; featureless, overexposed faces against underexposed backgrounds; vulgar and silly subtitles; impertinent lists of everybody employed in the film, from the star actress to the press agent's office boy, are only a few of the *gaffes* that American film factories are privileged to make. Conceit is rampant among your film makers; and good sense is about nonexistent. That is where Mr Chaplin scores; but Mr Harold Lloyd seems so far to be the only rival intelligent enough to follow his example. We shall soon have to sit for ten minutes at the beginning of every reel to be told who developed it, who fixed it, who dried it, who provided the celluloid, who sold the chemicals, and who cut the author's hair.[5] Your film people simply dont know how to behave themselves; they take liberties with the public at every step on the strength of their reckless enterprise and expenditure. Every American aspirant to film work should be sent to Denmark or Sweden for five years to civilize him before being allowed to enter a Los Angeles studio.

HENDERSON: . . . [C]an plays of conversation—"dialectical dramas"—like yours be successfully filmed?

SHAW: Barrie says that the film play of the future will have no pictures and will consist exclusively of subtitles.

HENDERSON: I wonder if conversation dramas are not on the wane: since the public, in countless numbers, patronizes, revels in, the silent drama.

SHAW: If you come to that, the public, in overwhelming numbers, is perfectly satisfied with no drama at all. But the silent drama is producing such a glut of spectacle that people are actually listening to invisible plays by wireless. The silent drama is exhausting the resources of silence. Charlie Chaplin and his very clever colleague Edna Purviance, Bill Hart and Alla Nazimova, Douglas Fairbanks and Mary Pickford and Harold Lloyd, have done everything that can be done in dramatic dumb show and athletic stunting, and played all the possible variations on it.[6] The man who will play them off the screen will not be their superior at their own game, but an Oscar Wilde of the movies who will flash epigram after epigram at the spectators, and thus realize Barrie's anticipation of more subtitles than pictures.

HENDERSON: If that is true, then why—since wit and epigram are your familiar weapons—why have none of your plays been filmed?

SHAW (*deadly resolute*): Because I wouldnt let them. I repeat that a play with the words left out is a play spoilt; and all those filmings of plays written to be spoken as well as seen are boresome blunders except when the dialogue is so worthless that it is a hindrance instead of a help. Of course, that is a very large exception in point of bulk; but the moment you come to classic drama the omission of the words and the presentation of the mere scenario is very much as if you offered the wire skeleton which supports a sculptor's modeling clay as a statue. Besides, consider the reaction on the box office. People see a Macbeth film. They imagine they have seen Macbeth, and dont want to see it again; so when your Mr Hackett or somebody comes round to act the play, he finds the house empty.[7] That is what has happened to dozens of good plays whose authors have allowed them to be filmed. It shall not happen to mine if I can help it.

1. Although Archibald Henderson (1877–1963), professor of mathematics at the University of North Carolina at Chapel Hill and author of three "authorized biographies" of Shaw (1911, 1932, and 1956), cast this "interview" in the form of a dialogue, he compiled it from Shaw's extended written responses to questions he had submitted, augmented by Shaw's own questions and answers.

2. German-born Ernst Lubitsch (1892–1947), known especially as a director of sparkling satiric comedies, began making films in America the previous year. Canadian-born Allan Dwan (1885–1981) directed more than four hundred Hollywood films.

3. Shaw misquotes *To the Memory of My Beloved, the Author, Mr. William Shakespeare* (1623) by Ben Jonson (ca. 1573–1637): "thou hadst small Latin and less Greek."

4. In Britain and America, Little Theatres were typically small, usually amateur operations that performed noncommercial drama. The Little Theatre movement was at its height during the first four decades of the twentieth century.

5. This prediction of a seemingly infinite number of credits has proved true, but they appear at the end, not the beginning, of films.

6. Edna Purviance (1894–1958) was Chaplin's leading lady in many silent comedies. William S. Hart (1870–1946) was a cowboy star. An internationally famous Russian stage actress, Alla Nazimova (1879–1945) began to appear in films in 1916. Douglas Fairbanks Sr. (1883–1939), known for his "athletic stunting," moved from Broadway to Hollywood to become a major star.

7. James K(eteltas) Hackett (1869–1926), born in America, was a leading man and romantic actor. Compare "Plays with Brains."

Shaw Not a Film Snob, but Cant Be a Dumb Dramatist

(*Daily News*, 26 February 1926/AG)

In your issue of the 23rd you say that "if distinguished and imaginative writers like Mr Shaw would cease to look on the moving picture contemptuously as a vulgar class of entertainment not worthy of their genius or literary dignity" certain beneficial results would follow.

I assure you I am entirely guiltless of any such senseless snobbery. I have recognized from the first the enormous importance, both artistically and morally, of the film, and I have never said or done anything inconsistent with that recognition.

But it does not follow from my appreciation of the possibilities of the dumb drama that I should become a dumb dramatist.

If Michael Angelo were now alive I have not the slightest doubt that he would have his letterbox filled with proposals from the great film firms to consecrate his powers to the delineation of Felix the Cat instead of painting the Sistine Chapel; but I think you will agree with me that his duty would lie in the direction of frescos and sculpture rather than of Los Angeles.[1]

Why can you not pardon me for thinking that a master playwright of seventy is better occupied in writing complete plays than fumbling with scenarios as a beginner?

Mr Harry Warner's public complaint of my inaccessibility is partly responsible for your misunderstanding.[2] But Mr Warner went on to describe how, regarding me as a national institution ("your Mr Shaw"), which no doubt I am, he took the phrase so literally that instead of simply writing to me, he approached the Foreign Office.

I regret that the Secretary of State for Foreign Affairs was too much occupied with Locarno or the proposed additions to the League of Nations to arrange a meeting for us; but, really, it was hardly his business.[3] A frontal attack may prove more successful.

1. The most popular cartoon character on the American screen before Mickey Mouse, Felix the Cat was introduced in 1914 by Australian-born animator Pat Sullivan (1887–1933) and achieved the apex of his fame in the 1920s.

2. Harry M. Warner (1881–1958) was president of Warner Brothers, founded in 1923 with his younger brothers Albert, Sam, and Jack L.

3. In 1925, in Locarno, Switzerland, Sir Austen Chamberlain (1863–1937), a winner of the Nobel Peace Prize that year, participated in a peace conference among former World War I enemies that established German boundaries. In 1926, Germany was admitted to the League of Nations.

Shaw Defends *The Big Parade*, Calls It a Fine Pacifist Study

(C/*World* [New York], 23 May 1926)

It is a pacifist film. It shews the excitement of people before they go to war and contrasts it with their subsequent discovery of its realities. I was astonished when a woman in the audience got up and shouted "Shame, there is no English soldier in the picture!"

It is an American film. If we produced a British picture would we put American soldiers in it?

Shaw in Film Debut Derides Movies

(C/X/SDI/*New York American*, 9 October 1926)[1]

I behaved just as any actor would, but when I saw the finished film it made me shout with laughter. Every single movement was hopelessly exaggerated. Thats the trouble with the American movies today. It's quite certain that the American producers havnt yet realized the enormous difference between acting on the film and acting on the stage: the technique is completely different.

The chief complaint I have to make against the American film is that the producers think that as long as it costs money it must be good. The backers of the American films are presumably all business men who think of art merely in terms of money.

It reminds me of the time Mr Goldwyn called on me here and talked to me for half an hour about himself.[2] He said he'd made so much money he didn't care about money at all. He asked me to write a scenario for him, declaring his sole future objective was to improve the level of art throughout the world.

I listened quietly to him, and at the end of the half hour, in bidding him goodbye, I remarked "I'm afraid, Mr Goldwyn, that we shall not ever be able to do business together. You see, youre an artist, and care only about art, while I'm only a tradesman and care only about money."

Griffith is an excellent example of the American producer of today. Unless he spends thousands and thousands of dollars he doesnt think his picture is any good. When he was over here I told him I could produce far better films than he could for about five cents each.

American producers have too much love for mob scenes, which dont increase the impressiveness of the film whatsoever.

Chaplin is about the only producer who seems to understand it. In The Gold Rush he produced a better effect by shewing men straggling along two at a time over the same pit of snow than he would have if he had covered the landscape with thousands of toiling men.[3]

Chaplin seems to me to be the best producer. He wastes very little, and when he gets his effect he snaps off at once. I realize, of course, that to prevent wastage is extremely difficult.[4]

I undertook to make a scenario of The Devil's Disciple. After I had written a practically complete history of the causes leading up to the American Revolution, together with vivid scenes from the Boston tea party, a close-up of Indians, and so forth, I found that the amount I'd written already needed about 50,000 feet of film and I hadnt got to the beginning of The Devil's Disciple itself. Someone said, I think it was Sir James Barrie, that without doubt the ideal film was one composed completely without subtitles, yet Oscar Wilde's Lady Windermere's Fan, although most people thought its interest lay solely in its sparkling dialogue, was a very fine piece.[5]

Individual producers seem to have a quite individual ability to make films seem like anything but the books or plays on which they are founded. One of Barrie's plays bore no resemblance whatever to the film, although I must admit I recognized the names of one or two of the characters.[6]

Sir Arthur Pinero's Iris had a happy ending tacked onto it. In the play a man threw his mistress out of his house. That was surely effective enough. In the film she was made to go out into the snow from the impressive mansion and walk straight across to her home in a terrible slum on the other side of the street, as though a house of the type she had left could possibly spring up in such a squalid neighborhood.

Yet I suppose it is possible for an author to recognize his work on the screen, [since] his characters are so strongly impressed on him.

A curious thing about the American producers is that they never seem to be confident they are achieving anything unless they go in the most roundabout way possible toward their objective, paying commissions right and left, such as twenty dollars to the policeman who directs them to my house.

1. Shaw composed this interview for H. K. Reynolds, under whose byline it appeared. While in Italy, Shaw participated in a short "Film Interview" that synchronized a phonograph and movie.

2. American film producer Samuel Goldwyn (né Goldfish, in Poland, 1882–1974).

3. *The Gold Rush* opened the previous year. Shaw seems to have forgotten the opening shots that show hundreds of prospectors climbing a snow-covered mountain.

4. Until relatively recently, the public was unfamiliar with Chaplin's film-making methods. He reshot takes, sequences, and entire scenes scores and sometimes hundreds of times. Since his method was largely improvisatory, he invented gags and stories while performing and shooting them, and he reshot sequences or scenes until he achieved the desired result. If he did not achieve it, he discarded the footage in favor of a new idea and sometimes abandoned the entire project. Shaw's comment on Chaplin's lack of wastage derives from Chaplin's refusal to have the camera linger after he achieved an effect. While one can only guess whether Shaw would have considered Chaplin's procedure wasteful, prodigal, or extravagant, one can conclude that Shaw's judgment derived from Chaplin's results.

5. Shaw may allude to Ernst Lubitsch's film version (1926) for Warner Brothers, but the play (1892) had also been filmed in England in 1919.

6. The play was *The Admirable Crichton*, the film *Male and Female*.

[Beauty but No Sex Appeal]

(F/Speech, London Pavilion Theatre, 18 November 1927)[1]

I have to introduce myself—Bernard Shaw—oh yes, t h e Bernard Shaw. I must also explain that I am an actual real animal; I am not the latest movietone illusion. I am no part really of the show. I have come here, if I may tell you a secret, because I want to get my knife into certain parts of this audience. I am very fond of the movies. I am what they call in America a "movie fan." Programs, however, are very often not to my liking. You see, the whole business of entertaining the public—a very important and responsible thing—is in the hands of the gentlemen whom we call the exhibitors, the gentlemen who keep all the picture palaces and select the films, except when they are selected for them by somebody else. But at any rate, they select the things that we have to look at afterwards.

I think you will admit that the men who discharge this extremely important function ought to be men of business, men of the world, and men of
sense. Unfortunately, they are nothing whatever of the kind. The pictures
attract a particular kind of man who is not a business man, a man of the
world, or a man of sense. He is an incurably romantic person. If you have
ever been to what is called a "trade show" and seen all the exhibitors
there, instead of saying "Oh, yes, here are men of the world, here are no
ordinary sort of persons," you would stare at them and say "Where on
earth did these people come from!" Their heads are full of the most
amazing things. They believe that the public are entirely occupied either
with wild adventures of the most extravagant kind or—what they believe
to be at least nine tenths of the whole attraction—with something they
call sex appeal. They are full of sex appeal. You may take the greatest
trouble to make the most beautiful and artistic film, but they say "Where
is the sex appeal?" And if there isnt what they call sex appeal, they simply wont believe that any people will go and see it.

You take one of these gentlemen and tell him "Are you aware that
large crowds go to hear the Dean of St Paul's preach, or that there is a
big building in Albermarle Street filled with people listening to scentific
lectures?[2] Are you aware that there are large halls all over the country
which are crowded to hear political speeches! They will reply "You
neednt talk to me about that. Where is the sex appeal?" Well, where is
the sex appeal of Dean Inge?[3] And you cannot do anything with them.
You bring them and shew them the most interesting films, and unless
there is what they call sex appeal they will not be converted. As a matter
of fact, the whole experience of the movies shews that sex appeal is a
thing that you may neglect almost altogether. Who are the two people
who in the very beginning of this cinematograph business have proved to
be the most universally attractive in the kinema? I should say Mr Charles
Chaplin and Miss Mary Pickford. There is no sex appeal in their films at
all. If you could get a picture that was perfect in sex appeal it would be
no use, for the reason that if it was made by a lady no lady would come
to see it, and if it was made by a man no man would go to see it. But
Miss Mary Pickford is just as popular, if not more popular, with women

as with men, which completely disposes of the idea that the attraction is what you call sex appeal. There is the attraction there of beauty and grace and interest and so on, but it is not sex appeal. On the contrary, the one painful part of these films, the part that always makes us pass it off with a laugh because we are used to it, or makes us feel slightly indelicate because we are looking at it, is the thing that is always put in at the end to satisfy the exhibitors.

The film may be dramatic, it may be entertaining, it may be a wonderful sketch of character, as you get from Mary Pickford and Charlie Chaplin, but no exhibitors care anything about that: you must compel Miss Pickford at the end of the film to exhibit herself being passionately kissed by a gentleman. They say Where is the sex appeal? You say Look at the last tableau; Miss Pickford is being kissed by somebody; and they accept that as the secret of the appeal. That is how you get a Pickford film off on the trade. Well, I find it extremely tantalizing to see another gentleman kissing Miss Pickford. If you would procure me the opportunity of kissing her, I might enjoy it, but when another gentleman is doing it I simply feel indelicate because I am looking on. If I had any prospects at my age of attracting the beautiful ladies of the film, I should not like to kiss them with a very large audience of people looking on. The very first thing I should demand is privacy.

No: it is a mistake. The really interesting films are independent of sex appeal. You will find before very long that, owing to the general public dissatisfaction and feeling of indelicacy at these final embraces, the final embraces will have to be cut out, and then what will become of the present film exhibitors. They will say There is no longer any film with sex appeal. What I think is important in an entertainment of this kind is not so much this or that feature in any particular form, but the whole program together. I believe my experience is probably that of most people. I go to a film show—mostly to listen to the music, which is extremely good as a rule—but I see the program. If I am bored by the program, I dont go for another fortnight. If I like a program I may go the next day. If you dont want to bore the public you must give them some sort of variety. But what sort of variety do they get in these eternal films of adventure and so-called sex appeal? There is always the gazette, a sort of newspaper on the screen and sometimes a very dull newspaper, but all the same it is popular. People like a program better for having a little interlude, and the attraction is not only the attraction of the news, because, as I say, that is sometimes rather dull. I myself do not enjoy seeing a perfectly uninteresting gentleman, whom I never heard of before, laying the foundation stone of a perfectly uninteresting building that is not yet built. The orchestra has to play with great spirit in order to carry me over these incidents. What I want to impress upon you is this: that the interest is very largely the interest of seeing something that really did happen as a relief from these wonderful films about thing which never could or did happen. It is all very well to go into dreamland for a moment, but you do want to keep your feet on the solid ground, and there is nothing so pleasant in the middle of all your romance as to have this moment of interest and realities.

The films which are to be shewn to the exhibitors who have been attracted here by the promise of a speech from me would be called by some people educational or instructional films. That description not only chokes off the trade exhibitor, but the whole world. Nothing would induce me to see an educational film, but on the other hand, I do want to see an interesting film, because if I know what is being shewn is something that has real interest and existence, then I like that immensely as a relief for a while from the romantic films. What we are going to shew you is a series of things that actually happen in nature. We are going to give a genuine moving piece of sex appeal: how a flower falls in love, how it opens its arms and invites embraces, and it is a beautiful thing to see. Miss Pickford could not beat it, if she went in for that kind of thing.

We will shew you several flowers. These are things that actually happen in nature, which you have never seen, probably, occur. We make them occur a little faster than they do in nature. They perhaps take several months in nature, and we will shew you the thing occurring in several seconds. But the thing actually does occur, and when you see it I believe you will agree with me that there is a quite extraordinary degree of beauty and grace and appeal in the thing. We will also shew you some diabolically ugly things. We have a film on the earwig here, and I hope you will look at it; but, at any rate, you will know that it is a real earwig. You will find out what happens to earwigs, and you will find out where they come from. I do not know whether we shall be able to shew you where they go to. If you saw it in an ordinary program with others, you would go away with your mind not only filled with romance, but, as a sort of contrast, you would know a lot about earwigs and you might find earwigs interesting. I do not know whether it is a desirable thing or not to do so, but at any rate the thing is interesting and what we are trying to persuade people is not to give a program consisting entirely of these things, because you can have too much of a good thing. I want them to stop having too much of the other sort of thing: I nearly said the bad thing, but of course I do not mean that.

When you have one thundering film like Ben Hur, there may not be room for anything else; but then in an ordinary program consisting of several pieces you will find it much more attractive to have one or two numbers of this kind, which we are going to shew you, something which appeals to the very strong love of nature that exists in the Englishman. He has a love of animals, he has a love of insects and flowers, he has a love of sport, a love or politics, and a love of religion; it is part of his character. The trade exhibitors know nothing about all this, except sex appeal, but we want to shew them that it takes all sorts of people to make a world, and they have gone on imagining—these exceptional and romantic men—that the whole world is full of the same kind of people. They think that the whole British public is like that. I want to impress on them that this is not so. The truth is that in many ways the exhibitors are very exceptional and morbid in their tastes and ought to see a doctor. They do not get the program that has two sorts of interest in it, and these exciting moments which they see so much in destroy the excitement by giving us nothing else the whole evening. There is so much excitement in the programs they give that at the end of two hours spent in a picture palace they could not shew you anything which would rouse the slightest emotions. If a few items of ordinary interest were put in for the sake of relief, then the romantic episodes [would] come out with their full value. They [would] have the effect of contrast; you are not worn out looking at them.

1. A conflation of VR of speech on a *Secrets of Nature* film in "Mr. Shaw as 'Movie Fan.' Advice to the Trade. A Plea for More Variety. Boredom of Sex Appeal," *Manchester Guardian*, 19 November 1927, and "A Relief from the Romantic Film," *Illustrated London News*, 3 December 1927, reprinted in *PP*. Although the latter admits it has excisions, which it does, it also has passages not in the former.

2. The Royal Institution, 21 Albemarle Street.

3. William Ralph Inge (1860–1954), Anglican clergyman, was dean of St. Paul's from 1911 to 1934. For many years he and the Shaws were personal friends.

[The Political Importance of Talking Films]

(HC to J. Ramsay MacDonald, 26 November 1927/CL 4)[1]

If they are still performing the Movietone Voices of Italy at the New Gallery, go and hear it even at the cost of missing a full dress debate. It is of e n o r m o u s political importance. The audience both sees and hears Mussolini ten times more distinctly and impressively than any audience has ever seen and heard u s; and the political party that wakes up to the possibilities of this method of lecturing will, if it has money enough, sweep the floor with its opponents.

Order the whole Labor Cabinet to go.

As the Movietone people have been very pressing about it to me, I have offered to do a stunt for them as a private experiment.[2]

G. B .S.

1. J(ames) Ramsay MacDonald (1866–1937), early member of the Fabian Society and Scottish labor leader, rose from poverty to head the Labour Party in 1911; in 1924 he became Britain's first Labour prime minister.

2. Shaw wrote from his new London residence, 4 Whitehall Court. In 1928, he did an "interview" for Movietone, in which he imitated Italy's fascist dictator Benito Mussolini.

What Is the Future for British Films?

(C/S/*British Film Journal*, January 1928)

There is a greater future for films than the Film Industry has yet grasped; and the British share in it will be just like any other national share: that is, as much as British brains and enterprise are able to grasp. Art knows nothing of frontiers.

Mr Shaw on the Cavell Film

(C/*Observer*, 19 February 1928)[1]

You might as well suggest that Sir George Frampton's monument should be demolished or veiled.[2] Are you to commemorate Edith Cavell in stone and not commemorate her in pictures? The only question to be considered is whether the film as a work of art is worthy of her. And you may take my word for it that it is.

You have a most moving and impressive reincarnation of the heroine by our greatest tragic actress, whose dignity keeps the whole story on the highest plane.[3] It has been planned and told by a young film poet who has been entirely faithful to his great theme: that of a woman who, at the risk of her life, kept a refuge for mercy and kindness in the midst of the European tornado of hate and terror.[4]

He has not betrayed her by a single stroke of bitterness or rancor, much less by any triviality of idle fiction. Both actress and author have felt, and will make us feel, that the law that Edith Cavell set above the military code and died for, is an infinitely higher law than the law of war and the conceit of patriotism.

The film can go to Germany as an English film without provoking any German to remind us that people who live in glass houses should not throw stones. It rebukes us all impartially, and will edify us impartially. I hope it will take its lesson to the ends of the earth.

1. A statement in response to British Foreign Secretary Sir Austen Chamberlain's demand that *Dawn* (1928) be suppressed. *Dawn* is about Edith Cavell, an English army nurse (1865–1915) whom the Germans executed in Belgium as a spy for having helped Allied prisoners to escape.
2. One of the best-known works of Sir George Frampton (1860–1928), a sculptor, is the Edith Cavell monument in St. Martin's Lane, London.
3. Sybil (later Dame Sybil) Thorndike (1882–1976), who played the title role in the first London production (1924) of *Saint Joan*.
4. The "film poet" was Herbert Wilcox (1892–1977), Irish-born producer-director.

Views on the Censorship

(*British Film Journal*, April–May 1928/TDO)

All the censorships, including film censorship, are merely pretexts for retaining a legal or quasi-legal power to suppress works which the authorities dislike. No film or play is ever interfered with merely because it is vicious. Dozens of films which carry the art of stimulating crude passion of every kind to the utmost possible point—aphrodisiac films, films of hatred, violence, murder, and jingoism—appear every season and pass unchallenged under the censor's certificates. Then suddenly a film is suppressed, and a fuss got up about its morals, or its effect on our foreign relations, or what not? Two glaring instances are now before the public. One of the best films ever produced as a work of pictorial art has for its subject a naval mutiny in the Russian Fleet in 1904, provoked by unbearable tyranny and bad food, followed by military operations against the citizens who sympathize with the mutineers.[1] The War Office and the Admiralty immediately object to it because it does not represent the quarterdeck and G.H.Q. as peopled exclusively by popular and gallant angels in uniform. It is suppressed. Then comes the Edith Cavell film. It is an extraordinarily impressive demonstration of the peculiar horror of war as placing the rules of fighting above the doctrine of Christ, and geographical patriotism above humanity. The demonstration is made through the genius of our greatest tragic actress. No matter: the film is at once suppressed on the ridiculous pretext that it might offend Germany. When the ban has to be removed under pressure of public opinion, the condition is imposed that the only incident which is sympathetic to Germany must be omitted. But the ban on the Potemkin film remains. It has nothing to do with the morals of the film; it is simply a move in class warfare. The screen may wallow in every extremity of vulgarity and villainy provided it whitewashes authority. But let it shew a single fleck on the whitewash, and no excellence, moral, pictorial, or histrionic, can save it from prompt suppression and defamation. That is what censorship means.

1. The mutiny, which occurred in 1905, is the subject of *Battleship Potemkin* (1925, called *Potemkin* in America), by Russian film and theatre director Sergei Mikhaylovich Eisenstein (1898–1948).

Bernard Shaw on Novelists and Films

(C/*Evening Standard*, 11 May 1928)[1]

Is that true? I should say they have always been keen on its possibility. Naturally they despise crude sob stuff and slapstick; but that applies to books as much as to films.

What is really dawning on them is that the screen is far more lucrative than the book.

It calls for more, much as the stage does. A novelist can describe all sorts of physical impossibilities without being found out by himself or anyone else. Both stage and screen bring him to the test of practice, and force him to use his brains as well as his imagination.

The real trouble is that ordinary fiction writers, when they try the stage or screen, will tomfool and write down to what they imagine to be the childishness and vulgarity of every art but their own. It is almost impossible to make novelists take the theatre seriously. They write stuff for it that no editor or publisher would look at.

1. Terence Atherton, a London journalist, compiled statements by Shaw, two film producers, and a film director and put them together as dialogue. Shaw's first comment responds to the assertion that most British writers have treated cinema contemptuously.

Mr Shaw and Mr Menjou

(C/X/VR/*New York Times*, 3 June 1928)[1]

MR SHAW: When I am rehearsing a play I go and see it thirty or forty times: not once do they ever get it a l l right, but each time there are one or two bits which I feel are just right, but it never happens that every-thing is right at the same performance. I can keep in my mind's eye each separate bit that has been right at the various rehearsals; and so I very seldom go to see my own plays. But in films, I suppose that with a suffi-cient number of trials you can get it all right?

MR MENJOU: Absolutely.

MR SHAW: But then I suppose you do not always have good directors: some directors may like all the bad bits and cut out all the good bits. That cannot happen on the stage, and so you can never have a real atrocity as you can in a film with a bad director.

MR MENJOU: I am very greatly interested in the new talking film process. In New York a few days ago I saw a film called The Tenderloin, in which both the two big dramatic moments—particularly where the heroine is subjected to a third-degree examination by the police—were done in talking films.[2] It was tremendous, and after that all the captions seemed dull and flat.

MR SHAW: That interests me a very great deal. Two or three days ago a huge wagon with batteries and various kinds of mechanism arrived at my front door in the country. It was this Movietone process, and they wanted me to talk and act in front of it. Well, I made an experiment to see what it could do. I tomfooled around the lawn and said all sort of things. . . .

Once before I was interviewed on a talking film. I behaved just as though it was on the stage. (Mr Shaw then got up, walked to the end of the room, puffed out his chest, strode round the room, raising his arm and lowering it.) That was what it looked like when it came out on the film. Everything was exaggerated to a ludicrous degree. They ought to have told me that before.

Mrs Patrick Campbell has had a film test, but she says that she was no good in it at all. The reason, of course, was that she had not been told to minimize every movement, because it comes out in so emphatic a way on the screen.

1. Reprinted from "Mr. G. B. Shaw Calls on Mr. [Adolphe] Menjou," *Daily Mail*, 21 May 1928.

2. This practice was typical of early talkies, including the first, *The Jazz Singer* (1927), which was a silent film with several talking sequences and sound musical numbers, such as "My Mammy," "Toot Toot Tootsie, Goodbye," and "Blue Skies."

[*Arms and the Man* and Early Talkies]

(P/X/HC to Rex Ingram, ca. late July–2 September 1928/BUL)[1]

I have been thinking over . . . the stage which your enterprise has reached at this moment; and if I were an entirely disinterested outsider I should say that classical comedy (as they now call Arms & the Man) is not your game just yet. Just think of it as if it were Molière's or Congreve's Way of the World, and you will see what I mean.[2]

G. B. S.

1. Ingram (né Reginald Ingram Montgomery Hitchcock, 1892–1950) was born in Ireland in 1911 and immigrated to the United States, where by 1916 he directed, wrote, and produced movies. In 1924, he established a studio in Nice, on the French Riviera. From 20 July to 2 September 1928, Shaw and his wife Charlotte were at Cap d'Antibes, on the Riviera, from which Shaw sent this card. In August, Shaw visited Ingram's studios to discuss the possibility of filming *Arms and the Man*.

2. On 20 October 1941 he again complained that "the technique of high comedy is quite beyond" Hollywood. See "[Revising *Arms and the Man* for Hollywood]."

[The Value of Film Rights and of Editing]

(X/TL to Matthew Edward McNulty, 4 December 1928/*CL* 4)[1]

For a long time I refused to allow my plays to be filmed because a screened play is a dead one in the ordinary theatre. But the value of my film rights commercially is so great that unless I realize them before I die my executors will sell them for twopencehalfpenny. Therefore I am now quite prepared to sell for five years the rights of those plays which have had a big revival lately and are consequently likely to go to sleep again for some years in the theatre. Besides, I am artistically interested. Owing to the fact that in filming you can select all the perfect bits from your rehearsals (every rehearsal hits off some passage to perfection) and piece them together into a perfect performance the screen can reach a point of excellence unattainable by the stage. Only, you must know which are the best bits. If, like many American producers, you prefer the worst, and piece t h e m together, the result is a sustained atrocity beyond the possibilities of a penny gaff.[2]

> ever
>
> G. B .S.

1. Shaw wrote to McNulty (1856–1943), a lifelong friend of Shaw since schooldays, from Ayot St. Lawrence.

2. A nineteenth-century term for a theatre, sometimes portable, sometimes improvised or partly so, in poor sections of London and other large cities, usually charging a penny or twopence for admission to see an inadequate company vigorously perform a melodrama.

Shaw Finds Talkies Opening New Field

(C/QI by Melchior Lengyel, *New York Times*, 19 May 1929)

The nicest thing about the film so far was that it kept its mouth shut. It would have been terrible if one had accompanied with words the stupidities which were played.

That was the only reason I did not permit the filming of my plays, because their greatest strength was in their dialogues, in what I had to say.

Here begins something new and interesting. It is not yet free from dry mechanism and it acts in the same manner as one winds the mechanism of a doll, but the mere fact [that] the importance of words in the film is recognized, will pave the way for writers because ultimately one will be able to distinguish between the good and the bad text.

That will secure for the films gifted playwrights the same as does the stage, although both are different in character.

The Living Talkies

(C/*Theatre Guild Magazine*, November 1929)[1]

It had been raining all the morning; fortunately the sun came out as I arrived. Mr Shaw seemed quite pleased to see me, even though I had at least once before stolen an interview with him.

"Of course the talkies have come to stay" he said, "and I cannot imagine any provincial theatre audience being satisfied with a £50 touring production when a £50,000 talkie is being shewn in a cinema. People wont accept third rate actors when they can see and hear 'stars' on the screen."

"But surely" I questioned "the flesh and blood actor will still be demanded by audiences?"

"No doubt," he said, "but not the same actors. The sooner that is realized the better. The ordinary actor, as such, is unsuitable for the talkies. The technique is quite different. Movie acting is mainly the art of not moving, as I discovered when I made my first picture. The first result was ludicrous and then I realized that I had to master a new method of moving. In order to produce a natural picture of myself I had to act in a quite unnatural way.

"The screen magnifies and intensifies and the clever movie actor knows this and does not appear on the ordinary stage. Mary [Pickford] and Douglas [Fairbanks] prefer to remain as the glorified beings that have been magnified by the camera. To see them as they really are would be like looking at them through the wrong end of a telescope.

"When the talkies came along the movie actor rushed in and, on the whole, was found to be a failure, for although he knows technically how to move he knows next to nothing about the voice. For the new medium we shall have to breed a race of talkie actors who have mastered the technique of moving and talking."

"Will you then allow your plays to be made into talking pictures?" I asked.

"Not until I am satisfied that there is a producer who also knows his job. I may then write a play especially for the talkies, although I see no reason why *The Apple Cart*, for instance, should not be produced exactly as it stands."[2]

I asked if he had seen any color films. He said "Although one or two have been fairly satisfactory, I do not believe that there is any general desire for color. People are used to black and white."

Shaw then summarized his views on the talkies in the following letter to me:

I have satisfied myself by a successful personal experiment that it is possible to reproduce dramatic dialogue such as I write, the effect being as convincing as when it is spoken on the stage.[3]

It has been established already that stage action can be reproduced effectively on the screen.

Stage vision can be reproduced in monochrome; and the absence of color is not only pardoned by the audience, but forgotten. The likelihood of the present two-color and three-color attempts at chromatic photography becoming reasonably truthful may therefore be left out of the discussion.

Plays and operas can, in view of the foregoing propositions, be successfully reproduced as Talkies (or Singies) as soon as the following conditions are fulfilled:

That companies of performers who have mastered the special technique of motion, speech, and song required for reproduction by instruments which greatly magnify them and intensify them (neither our movie stars nor our stage actors are qualified in this way a s s u c h: in fact they are disqualified) will be available.

That all patentees of apparatus be drowned, shot, sent to St Helena, or otherwise effectively excluded from the studios, the moment they demonstrate the practicalities of their inventions.[4]

That a new race of artistic producers who understand the new technique involved by magnification, and who know good work from bad when they see it and hear it, a n d w h o d o n t p r e f e r t h e b a d, be discovered and placed in control of the originating performances.

1. Interview by G. W. Bishop. A different version of this interview, titled "A Walk and a Talk with Mr. Shaw," appeared in the *Observer*, 8 September 1929.

2. *The Apple Cart* was produced at the Malvern Festival on 14 June and transferred to London on 17 September. The Theatre Guild would give its American premiere in New York on 24 February 1930. The Malvern Festival, founded and managed by Sir Barry Jackson (1879–1961) and Roy Limbert (1893–1954), from 1929 to 1939 and after World War II in 1949, was primarily a Shaw festival. It produced twenty-two of his plays, six of them for the first time in England, one a world premiere.

3. On 27 July 1927, the DeForest Phonofilm Company, synchronizing film and phonograph, recorded the cathedral scene from *Saint Joan*, starring Sybil Thorndike.

4. Napoleon was banished to St. Helena in 1815.

A Charming Boy Aged 73 Who Talks Mostly about the Talkies

(C/X/QI by Sewell Stokes, *Good Housekeeping*, December 1929)

I'm particularly keen on Talkies. I'll tell you why.

It is not possible to get a perfect production of a play on the stage. Or if one does manage, after careful rehearsal, to get it nearly perfect on a Monday night, who can tell what it will be like on Tuesday? No actor can repeat a performance exactly. One night he may be good, the next less good. But the films have an advantage. Through them one can actually get a perfect production. A man like Chaplin can spend as much time as he likes making a bit of film perfect. In the end all he has to do is to join up the bits, and the result is a perfect production which will stand forever.

Before the Talkies came, the films did not need my plays, or anybody else's. They bought plays, I know. But why? A play is made up of dialogue. By the time it was filmed all the dialogue had been taken out of it, so that the plays which were filmed successfully could not have been plays at all.

The trouble is that the people who ask amateurs to act or talk never explain to them the one important fact: that is, the speed at which they must act or talk. . . . You see, one doesnt need to act for the films at all. One only has to move slightly. Even one's thoughts are turned by the camera into movements. An actor only has to think to convey an impression on the screen. I dont suggest that the majority of film stars are capable of thinking for themselves. But a producer can tell them what to think!

[Shaw's Plays on Film]

(P/TL to a Mr. Messulam, ca. 1930s/BL 50522)[1]

A perfect [motion] picture is not possible. At all events I cannot design one.

I do not write for the approval of all picturegoers in all towns and in all spheres of life, but for people who have a cultivated taste for the particular class of work that my name is identified with.

I shall most certainly not agree to have my work meddled with by an American or American-trained expert. If you want his work you need not come to me. If you want mine there is no occasion for his services. On the whole, I think you had better conclude that you have come to the wrong shop.

I am none the less obliged to you for your proposal.

1. In a letter of 30 September 1942 to Shaw, J. A. Oldridge of Oxford reported he had acquired this letter, of which he gave the text but no date. Since this is a business letter, Shaw probably signed it "G. Bernard Shaw."

The Cinema as an Art Form

(To Huntly Carter, 1 January 1930/CL 4)[1]

The question has no meaning for me, as art is to me only a method of intelligible or sensible expression, and art forms are processes to be carried out by instruments under the control of the artist. Art for art's sake is rather like fox hunting or skating, which have no sense except as ways of procuring food or moving from place to place, but are continued for fun by people who dont eat foxes and who, after hours of skating, take off their skates at the spot where they put them on, without having traveled in the meantime further than the opposite side of the pond.

Drama is a method of rearranging the higgledy-piggledy happenings of actual life in such a way as to make them intelligible and thinkable. Its forms, processes, and instruments include the stage, the screen, the camera, the microphone, the actor, and all the other things by which the final effect desired is wrought on the senses of the audience. There is nothing new in the art of drama; but a cinema is a new art form like a new instrument added to the orchestra or a new verse form, like that in Bridges' Testament of Beauty.[2] It is available, of course, for scientific demonstration also, as when it makes the month's growth of a pea visible within a few seconds.

Also it is practiced for fun like hunting. In the palmy days of acting, people found the declamation of an actor so curious and agreeable that they would crowd to hear him ranting through plays in which there was less sense than there is meat in fox.

In short, I dont quite see why you should boggle at the description of the cinema as an art form. All I can do is to make my own view clear.

[G. Bernard Shaw]

1. In this QI, Carter asked: "(1) In your opinion should the Cinema fulfil a social function for the community? (2) Do you know of any particular form that would raise the level of interpretative power and with it the level of achievement? (3) If an 'Art Form,' do you mean a form determined by the æsthetic of technique, or by a natural æsthetic? As in the 'Secrets of Nature' pictures which reveal natural objects putting on their own form and color." Carter published Shaw's response in *The New Spirit in the Cinema* (1930) under the title used above.

2. In *The Testament of Beauty* (1929), a poem in four books, Robert Bridges (1844–1930) employs what he calls "neo-Miltonic syllabics."

[Should a Theatre Company Produce Talking Films? (I)]

(C/X/TL to Lawrence Langner, 15 February 1930)[1]

Do you think there is any serious chance of The Guild doing anything with Arms and the Man as a talkie? Goldwyn is pressing me about it; and Stern cables to ask whether he may name $150,000 as my price in a deal which is proposed.[2] There is no immediate prospect of my entertaining these proposals; for Goldwyn wants to cut my play down to forty minutes; and I suspect some of the other applicants of wanting to film, not Arms and the Man, but The Chocolate Soldier.[3] Also Mary Pickford is very keen to do Cæsar and Cleopatra; and, generally speaking, my film market is getting excited. Meanwhile my hands are tied by our understanding about the Guild having a shot at talkie producing; but it is obvious that on coming to close quarters with such a very laborious and expensive new departure, you may find it quite impractical—if, indeed, you have not already done so. How does the matter stand? I am in no hurry; but I cannot wait unless I see a reasonable chance of something happening.[4]

I have to thank you very cordially for your reception of Cecil Lewis on my introduction. He was greatly gratified by the way you treated him, especially as his head is full of schemes of film work on my plays.[5]

> Faithfully
> G. Bernard Shaw

1. Published in Langner's *G. B. S. and the Lunatic* (1963). A transcript of the letter (DHL) reveals Shaw's address, 4 Whitehall Court, and his signature.

2. Benjamin H. Stern (1874–1950), an authority on international copyright law, was a partner in the New York law firm Stern and Reubens, Shaw's American lawyers.

3. The operetta *The Chocolate Soldier* (*Der tapfere Soldat*, 1908), music by Oscar Straus (1879–1954), libretto by Rudolf Bernauer (1880–1953) and Leopold Jacobson (b. 1878), was an unauthorized adaptation of *Arms and the Man*. Shaw objected to it but agreed not to sue for plagiarism if no names or dialogue from *Arms and the Man* were used and no suggestion were made that the operetta was adapted from his play, but he allowed such phrases as "as suggested by one of Mr. Bernard Shaw's comedies" or "with apologies to Mr. Bernard Shaw for an unauthorized parody."

4. On 7 March, Langner responded that while several movie companies were willing to finance the Theatre Guild's filming some of Shaw's plays, they were unwilling to do so unless Shaw altered his financial demands and gave them the

right to change the plays. The Guild therefore declined Shaw's proposal. Compare Shaw's letter to Gabriel Pascal, 18 November 1946.

5. Cecil Lewis (1898–1997), one of the four founders of the BBC (British Broadcasting Corporation) in 1922, would soon direct the screen versions of *How He Lied to Her Husband* (1931) and *Arms and the Man* (1932) for British International Pictures. Although he botched them, Shaw faulted the producers, not him.

"Film Censorship Must Go," Says G. B. S.

(C/*Evening Standard*, 17 February 1930)[1]

There is no end to the craziness of this censorship business. The name of a common and responsible public man is appended to the certificate to reassure the public of their value, but the Censor can pass through life without ever seeing a film.

The actual inspection is done by three examiners who sit in a room with three films going simultaneously, each examiner wanting to look at the other's film when his own is unbearably dull.

All they have to do is to see that certain subjects are not mentioned, a job in the competence of anyone worth £5 a week—if you leave out the torture of looking at films all day and every day.

I can only ask Mr Edward Shortt publicly what he supposes he is paid for, and what difference it would make to public morals if his office were abolished?[2]

One film I saw exhibited in a London cinema I could stand no longer; I fled from the theatre in disgust.

When I find an official who is entrusted with the arbitrary control of the picture theatre allowing unlimited liberty to one type of film and refusing to allow honest and decent social welfare films to be exhibited, wasting the heavy expenditure of those who have made them, and stigmatizing them as immoral persons, then I appeal to public opinion to sweep that official and his powers and his department to the dustbin.

1. Statement on the British Board of Censors's ban of *The Night Patrol*, a film made by Elizabeth Baxter. See the next selection for further commentary on this film.

2. From 1919 to 1922, Shortt (1862–1935) served as chief secretary for Ireland, and in 1922 became home secretary. From 1929 to 1933, he was the second president of the British Board of Film Censors.

Mr Shaw on Film Censorship: "Efficient for Evil"

(C/*Times*, 17 February 1930)

May I call attention to the latest example of the manner in which our censorships, with the best intentions, safeguard the very evils they are supposed to prevent?

A lady has made it her business to help homeless and penniless people who spend their nights in the streets and make the Embankment a general address for misery. She has found that many of the men have tramped up to London in the belief, not exactly that its streets are paved with gold, but that there is plenty of employment to be had here at higher wages than in the provinces. She also finds that young women come up in answer to advertisements in helpless ignorance of the existence, much less the address, of the Travelers' Aid and other Societies for the protection of women and children from White Slave agents.

The lady has taken a very sensible step, the only effective one within her means. She has had typical nightly scenes on the Embankment filmed and set in the framework of a simple story shewing a miner leaving his family to better them by seeking work in London, and presently finding himself on the Embankment desiring nothing more than to get back to his home and his old job in the country. The film also shews a girl decoyed to London by a White Slaver's advertisement. She is fortunate enough, after being drugged and carried on board a ship bound for the Continent, to escape before anything worse has happened to her, and to be directed to the proper quarter for protection and advice.

Obviously the exhibition of such a film throughout the country would be extremely unwelcome to the White Slavers, and would check the flow of unwanted men to London. To the stupefaction of the lady and her charitable colleagues the film was refused a licence. They came to me and put the case before me. As I knew by what I had seen of licensed films that it was quite possible to exploit night scenes and incidents of the White Slave traffic in an objectionable way I asked to see the film. I was at once invited to a private exhibition, only to find that even this could not be given without permission. Finally, however, I saw it where the Censor's writ did not run; and I can testify that there is not an incident or suggestion in it that could not be exhibited in a Sunday school, the pictures being as innocent in their execution as in their intention.

I asked what reason the examiners who do the work of censorship had given for their decision. I was told that they had relented so far as to license the story of the miner "for adults," which seemed to me madder, if possible, than its total prohibition. But they would not license the story of the girl on any terms, their reason being that they thought domestic servants were badly wanted in London, and that the film might discourage girls from coming to help London out of that difficulty. How girls could be discouraged from traveling by an advertisement of the means by which they could do so in safety was not explained.

As I never make a public grievance of a matter that can be quietly remedied by a reasonable representation to the responsible authority, I persuaded the owners of the film to say nothing until I had written privately to Mr Edward Shortt, who lately succeed the late T. P. O'Connor as Film Censor.[1] As he had survived a term of office as Irish Secretary, and had acted as Home Secretary subsequently, I had no doubt that his experience and good sense would at once convince him that his examiners had blundered, and that he would set matters right without any public fuss.

His reply is that he has now seen the film, and agrees with the judgment of the examiners, not for the reasons given by them, but because it is a rule of his department to allow no reference to the White Slave traffic or to drugs. I could hardly believe my eyes as I read this amazing statement of policy. The most lavish and costly displays of the allurements held out by White Slavers to young women, and by them to their patrons, are licensed without demur, and thereby effectually protected and sanctioned. Licensed scenes of what is politely called exhibitionism have become cinema specialities: one which I cannot describe in your columns was shewn recently in a first rate West End picture house. But when a film is made to shew girls the risk they run of being kidnapped by White Slavers, and to make known to them the address of a society which exists to make such kidnapping impossible, the Censor suppresses it. It is as if the railway companies were to exclude the staff of the Travelers' Aid Society from their arrival platforms whilst giving every facility to the White Slave agents on the very acceptable condition that the real nature of their business must not be disclosed.

I know, of course, that as the series of considered moral judgments for which the public look to the Film Censor are absurdly impracticable, his business reduces itself to the enforcement of a few rules of thumb through which any unscrupulous person can drive a coach and six, though they are intolerably obstructive and injurious to conscientious authors; but this particular rule seems to me beyond all bearing except by those who have pecuniary interests in the White Slave and drug traffics. It convinces me, as one who frequents picture houses, and knows the lengths to which they go in the direction which the censorship exists solely to bar, that it is quite useless for good and terribly efficient for evil.

As Mr Shortt cannot be questioned in Parliament, which has no control of him or his emoluments, and as my private appeal to him has been in vain, I am obliged to resort to the Press through its most influential organ.

The title of the film is *The Night Patrol*; and the lady's name is Miss Baxter.

1. Thomas Power O'Connor (1848–1929), Irish journalist and M.P. for the Irish Party, employed Shaw as music critic for the *Star*, which he founded in 1887, from 1888 to 1890. In 1917, he was appointed the first president of the British Board of Film Censors, a position he held until his death.

G. B. S.—"Talkie" Prophet

(C/SDI/*Today's Cinema*, 21 February 1930)[1]

"So far as the recording and reproducing are concerned, the 'talkies' could hardly be bettered.

"It may take seven or eight years" he said, "but by that time an artist who is exclusively a 'talkie' artist, as opposed to a stage or silent film artist, will have been evolved.

"Let producers stop trying to improve machinery that is already excellent, and concentrate on the human side of 'talkie'-making.

"As soon as the present boom commenced, I made a personal appearance on the talking screen. Since that experience I have become convinced that a person's speech and actions can be reproduced as effectively on the screen as if he himself were addressing the audience.

"But that person must know how to speak.

"I consider that my own 'talkie' was successful because I am accustomed to making speeches in public. 'Talkies' made by Ramsay MacDonald and Mr Lansbury were successful for the same reason.[2]

"Artists must learn to speak as well as these two gentlemen. But they must also learn to act as well as film stars have acted on the silent screen.

"At present very few are able to combine these qualities. Stage artists sing and speak well on the 'talkies,' but can only act in a stagelike manner. Film artists act as required, but cannot speak correctly.

"A new kind of artist exclusively devoted to this type of entertainment has to be discovered before 'talkies' can be seen at their best.

"I do not want in the least to see stereoscopic effects in the cinemas" he said.[3] "It would not, I think, be any improvement on present methods.

"What I want is to see the evolution of actors and actresses who are exclusively 'talkie' stars."

1. Shaw composed this self-interview as an article. I have omitted his quotations from "What the Films May Do to the Drama," reprinted above.

2. George Lansbury (1859–1940), a lifelong socialist, would be a leader of the Parliamentary Labour Party from 1931 to 1935.

3. Stereoscopy aims to create three-dimensional effects.

The Censorship Scandal

(C/*New Leader*, 28 February 1930)

It is a political case.[1] British Capitalism is at war with Russian Communism and with British Socialism. Communism has given the Russian outlook on life an enormous superiority, which Capitalism is trying to paint black by a torrent of calumny. It will not even allow artistic merit to a Russian film. The other day the Daily Telegram had the audacity to describe Russian films as "crude." The Potemkin film is banned solely because it is Russian, and because it appeals to workingclass sympathy against Czarist militarism. The rule is "as much debauchery as you like, but no proletarianism."

1. The London County Council banned *Mother* (1926), directed by one of the Soviet Union's great filmmakers, Vsevolod I. Pudovkin (1893–1953), adapted from the novel *Mother* (1907) by Maxim Gorky (pseudonym of Aleksei Maksimovich Peshkov, 1868–1936). The LCC censors did not see the film; nor did Shaw, who had seen *Potemkin*, which had been banned for similar reasons.

Shaw Asserts Theatre Is Lost, Signs for Films

(*New York Herald Tribune*, 8 August 1930/TDO)[1]

The poor old theatre is done for!

All my plays will be made into "talkie" films before long. What other course is open for me?

The theatre may survive as a place where people are taught to act, but apart from that there will be nothing but "talkies" soon. I stood out against the silent film, it is true, but that was because the silent film is no good to me. I have certainly made no prolonged stand against the talking film, which is a different proposition altogether.

I cant tell which of my plays is likely to be filmed next. Conceivably it may be Arms and the Man. I dont know.

The reason I took my own contract with me to the film people is that I have always drawn up my own contracts and have taken them with me when it comes to sign them. My experiences have been that the average lawyer has no idea how to draw up a contract which is outside the usual run of business, so I do my own.[2]

1. Statement on signing a contract with British International Pictures to produce his one-act play *How He Lied to Her Husband* as a talking film. Its first showing was 12 January 1931. Narrative portions of this article are omitted.

2. See appendix.

G. B. S. Hits Hollywood

(C/*Sunday Dispatch*, 1 March 1931)[1]

There is not a word of truth in it, but if the writer really had the inside knowledge of Elstree [Studios] he pretends to, and had told the truth, it would not have amused anybody. Still, he might have written something interesting; for the film is a bit of a curiosity, as its difficulties have never been faced in Hollywood.

The American experts insist on frequent changes of scene and long intervals of silence during which the film is a movie and not a talkie. I have repeatedly challenged them to reproduce my plays on the screen just as they are produced on the stage. They declare it impossible: they could work only on condition of being allowed to adapt the play to their technique instead of adapting their technique to the play.

British International Pictures, with Mr Cecil Lewis as producer [i.e., director], accepted the challenge and achieved the feat that Hollywood had found impossible; and I am glad to hear that you find the result agreeable. The play, How He Lied to Her Husband, was selected because it pushed the test to the utmost.

Of course the movie fan critics, who are incapable of following closely knit dialogue and know no other dialect than Californian, are hopelessly left behind after three sentences, and fill their papers with their dismayed bleatings in that tongue, but they have not been supported by the seriously qualified critics, nor by the intelligent section of cinemagoers who want to hear some real dramatic talk from the talkies instead of a ha'porth of back chat and novelet gush to £100,000 worth of dissolving views.

I am wondering what Hollywood will say when it is asked, not merely for half an hour of real unintermitted comedy like How He Lied to Her Husband, but for Strange Interludes and Back to Methuselahs and Hamlets.[2]

1. An American newspaper commented that the talking movie version of his one-act play *How He Lied to Her Husband* was "the world's biggest flop."

2. *Strange Interlude* (1928) is a nine-act play by Eugene O'Neill, in which characters speak long "interior monologues" of their thoughts; its first New York performance, by the Theatre Guild, lasted almost five hours. In 1932, MGM filmed *Strange Interlude*, cutting it to one hour and fifty minutes. It starred Canadian-born Norma Shearer (1900–1983) and Clark Gable, both very popular. MGM advertised it as "the film in which you hear the characters THINK!" Shaw designed *Back to Methuselah* for performance on five consecutive evenings, and its first British performances at Malvern (1923) and in London (1924) conformed to his design, but he let the Theatre Guild present its world premiere in New York (1922) in three evenings.

[Theatre People's Obtuseness to Talking Films]

(C/X/QI by Hayden Church, *Sunday Express*, 1 March 1931)[1]

I am not interested in any particular phase of the talkies. I am interested in the enormous fact that the method of projecting drama and acting has been discovered which reduces our cheap shabby, half-visible, half-audible old stage method to absurdity.

And our theatre people are still blinking at it, and saying it will not last because the public like the real thing. As if Charlie Chaplin were not ten times more real to us than any stage actor in the world!

If this is true of Charlie Silent, what will Charlie Talking be? It is pitiable to hear our old theatre managers prophesying nonsense on their way to oblivion through the bankruptcy court.

1. Published under the title "G. Bernard Shaw Talks About Love, Sex, Charlie Chaplin and Why Old Men Don't Matter."

Theatre Managers and Film Rights

(*Author*, Spring 1931/*TDO*)[1]

An author who gives a manager or publisher any rights in his work except those immediately and specifically required for its publication or performance is for business purposes an imbecile. As 99 percent of English authors and 100 percent of American ones are just such imbeciles, managers and publishers make a practice of asking for every right the author possesses: translation rights, world rights, dramatization rights, and film rights for the whole duration of the copyright at a fraction of their market value. Imbeciles are always afraid to say no; and the result is that the concession of such rights soon becomes customary: with the imbeciles. The first time I ever negotiated the London production of one of my plays the acting manager who had been told to settle with me

remarked pleasantly "Of course you will give us the American rights."
I grinned and replied "Of course I wont." He grinned and dropped the
subject. If I had been an imbecile I should have assented nervously.

That is how the thing is done. Authors who have not brains enough to
understand their legal and economical position, nor character enough to
take care of their own interests, had better put themselves in the hands of
the professional association to which they should belong (in Britain the
Society of Authors) and allow it to dictate their agreements and collect
their royalties. But many authors are not intelligent enough in the real
world (they are all perfect Einsteins in the realm of fiction) to join an
association; consequently they undersell their more sensible colleagues
so disastrously that the professional association finds the market spoilt
by the competition of the nerveless and spineless blacklegs who will take
anything that is offered to them and grant any concession that is asked.
Thus we find the Authors' League of America letting down its members
heavily by conceding in its minimum basic agreement half the film proceeds as of right to the theatrical managers: a monstrous and perfectly
gratuitous betrayal of its members. Still, it is better for an American
imbecile to be let down halfway by the Authors' League than to be let
down to the ground by his own greed for production or publication, and
his own timidity. In the same way, though it is never worth an agent's
while to stand out for the top price which an author of full business competence can obtain for himself, yet for an imbecile it is better to make a
middling bargain through an agent than a very bad one without an agent.

Nothing will save the majority of authors from themselves except a
ruthlessly tyrannical Professional Association having no other interest
than to keep up the market to its highest practical possibilities. And this
is very difficult to establish as long as authors work separately for their
own hands (usually hands with no business muscle in them) and never
dream of considering the interests of their profession as a whole when
they are driving their little bargains with their exploiters, who naturally
do most of the driving. It is pitiable to see a body of professional men on
whom the Copyright Acts have conferred a monopoly of enormous value

unable to do for themselves what is done by porters and colliers and trade unionists generally with no monopoly at all at their backs.

1. Statement in reply to the question "Has the theatre manager any moral claim to an interest in the film rights?"

My First Talkie

(*Malvern Festival Book*, [August] 1931/ST)

To the uninitiated general patrons of the Talkies the little film How He Lied to Her Husband is a talkie like any other talkie. To those behind the scenes it is an experiment. Like all playwrights, I have had many proposals from the great film corporations for the screening of my plays, some of them tempting enough commercially. In the days of the Movies the objection to these proposals was that my plays were made to be spoken and could be of no use as silent plays, no matter how ingeniously they were patched by scraps of printed dialogue thrown on the screen as subtitles. When the Talkies arrived the situation was changed. It became possible for the screen not only to shew my plays, but to speak them. The rejected proposals were renewed.

But when we came down to the tacks, I found that the film corporations were nearly as far as ever from real play screening. The only business they had mastered was the Movie business; and their notion of a screened play was really only a Movie with spoken subtitles. The only use they had for a play was to rearrange it as a Movie in which the actors were occasionally heard as well as seen; and the movie stars, instead of putting drama into their voices, put it, as they were accustomed to, into their facial expression and gesture, and then repeated the words by rote, unmeaningly and often very discordantly. Though they had acquired to perfection the special art of moving for the lens, they had no idea of the equally special art of speaking for the microphone.

In this phase the talkie art was quite useless to me. My plays do not consist of occasional remarks to illustrate pictures, but of verbal fencing matches between protagonists and antagonists, whose thrusts and ripostes, parries and passados, follow oneanother much more closely than thunder follows lightning. The first rule for their producers is that there must never be a moment of silence from the rise of the curtain to its fall. Hollywood would not hear of such a condition: it was, they said, impossible. To cut out half my dialogue, in order to insert dozens of changing pictures between the lines of what was left, seemed to them quite indispensable. So we parted with reciprocal assurances of the highest consideration, but: nothing doing.

It was, I think, the great success of the talking films in which Mr George Arliss appeared that first shook the Hollywood superstition. Mr Arliss's performances proved that a good play could be a good play, and good acting good acting, on the screen exactly as on the stage. British International Pictures resolved to try an experiment in the new manner; and I placed How He Lied to Her Husband at their disposal for the purpose. Mr Cecil Lewis, a playwright and stage producer, keen on developing the talkie dramatically, and free from Hollywood superstitions, undertook the direction.

The result can be seen and heard at the Malvern Picture House during the Festival. The points for connoisseurs are (a) that the dialogue is continuous from end to end except when Mr Gwenn purposely makes a silence more dramatic than words could be, and (b) that as the entire action takes place in the same room, the usual changes from New York to the Rocky Mountains, from Marseilles to the Sahara, from Mayfair to Monte Carlo, are replaced by changes from the piano to the sideboard, from the window to the door, from the hearth rug to the carpet.[1] When the husband arrives he is not shewn paying his taxi, taking out his latchkey, hanging up his hat, and mounting the stairs. There is no time for that sort of baby padding when the action of a real play is hastening to its climax. Yet I do not think anyone will miss it. It will seem incredible that only the other day Hollywood declared that such things are the life and soul of the film.

When How He Lied was produced in London the young film fans complained that the conversation of my characters was such as had never been heard except in oldfashioned XIX century superliterary books. The poor fellows had never read anything but a Hollywood subtitle. They could not be persuaded that English people really talk like that. My Malvern patrons will know better.

    1. Edmund Gwenn (1877–1959), who had acted in Shaw's plays at the Court Theatre and elsewhere, became a famous film actor. His most popular role was Santa Claus in *Miracle on 34th Street* (1947), for which he won an Oscar. In *How He Lied to Her Husband* he played the Husband.

[Adapting *Arms and the Man* to the Screen]

(X/HL to Cecil Lewis, 18 April 1932/CL 4)[1]

Please send the pages I have skipped to Whitehall Court.

The changes—the garden as a relief to the library and the absence of Louka from the stage during the scene of Petkoff & the photograph—are excellent. The garden should have two talking places and an urn or something for Louka to dump the letters on and perhaps for occasional posing. A glade with a statue would be beyond the Petkoffs; but a well is a useful property. Anyhow, do not have the Louka-Sergius duet on the same bench as the Raïna-Bluntschli one: the former needs more privacy and romance—less obviously under the house windows.

I am not against your overlays on principle: I am quite eager to try them and confident of their effectiveness in the right place.[2] But they have to be very carefully contrived; and as I have noted at Petkoff's entry in his shirtsleeves, I feel sure that an overlay spoken by a person whose presence has not been visually impressed immediately before is hopeless unless the overlaid one is a ghost.

Also the balance between the full sets and close-ups should be carefully watched. I think How He Lied suffered from the audience not seeing the whole room often enough. A screenplay all close-ups and groups and corners is rather like a melodrama all asides. Keep the audience well in mind of the whole room, the whole garden, even the whole landscape in which the close-ups take place. . . .

Remember that in a movie the faces alone matter; but in a talkie the voices are urgent. Raïna must be a soprano and Louka a contralto. Bluntschli must have a dry voice and Sergius a ringing one. If Nature has not made the difference Art must supply it.

GBS

1. Cecil Lewis, director of *Arms and the Man*, wrote the screenplay and sent pages to Shaw for approval as he composed them. The day before, Shaw wrote to him from Ayot St. Lawrence, "If I had time I would half rewrite the play and invent at least fifty more changes of scene" (quoted in headnote to this letter in *CL 4*).

2. "Overlays" are voice-overs.

Relation of the Cinema to the Theatre

(QI by Huntly Carter, 9 May 1932/TDO)[1]

Do you believe that the cinema and the theatre have different functions? That is, a difference seen at once in the finished production? And that the cinema is trying to perform the function of the theatre, and the theatre will ultimately be absorbed?

No. Both of them are instruments. The cinema has the wider range of the two, and can be used for spreading news, demonstrating natural history and biology, exhibiting surgical operations, and so forth; but when it performs plays its function is the function of the theatre.

In your opinion would the theatre have been better without the cinema? Or has the cinema helped the theatre by taking over objects and agents of representation that are beyond the limits of the theatre; by calling attention to theatrical entertainment, creative, intellectual, and cultural, which is beyond the province of the cinema; and by emphasizing the true character of cheap and shoddy and unclean stage plays, like the Aldwych farces, that have been screened?[2]

Certainly not. Theatres before the cinema came were, and still are, uncomfortable, unhealthy, ridiculously expensive, and ruinous to their lessees. The comparative comfort of the picture houses, their lucrativeness in spite of the prodigious sums expended on films, their superior cultural and intellectual range, are making the old theatres and their limits impossible. Even in its worst wallowings in the mud the cinema is incomparably more brilliant than the theatre.

In your view can the "talkie" cinema continue to ape the theatre with any advantage to itself? If it swallowed the theatre could it continue to live?

The talkie does not ape the theatre any more than a Rolls Royce apes a Victorian four wheeled cab. It just plays it off the stage when it is well handled. When its technique is mastered, and we have highly skilled and thoroughly professionalized actors instead of experienced amateurs—to say nothing of inexperienced ones—ninetynine percent of the present occupation of the theatre will be gone; and the remaining one percent will consist in training the public to appreciate the novelties of the cinematic pioneers.

Can each take its own path without injury to the other? Do you believe that there is a line of development by which the cinema can reach completeness? And a line of development by which the theatre can reach a perfection (a higher level of interpretative power) hitherto unattained? Let us say both from an entertainment point of view, using the term in the best sense.

Nothing in art can reach completeness: the horizon is always remote. There is plenty of room for mechanical development in the theatre. The managers of most of our theatres do not know what a hydraulic bridge is, or a rolling or revolving stage, or a microphone. I still need only "four boards and a passion" to hold an audience; but it is silly that I should be limited to them at this time of day.[3]

Cooperation: Do you believe that anything is to be gained in the future if the cinema and the theatre came to act together as free self-acting units? Through a system of voluntary combination by which the theatre expressed the finer and more intimate stages of a vast theme, say the political plotting and planning leading to a great war; and the cinema the immense stages, say, the representation of the great tragedy of the war itself? Say your own plays for the theatre and the far wider issues, political and social, which they imply, for the cinema?

I do not foresee a mixed genre. I consider the cinema far more capable of fine and intimate work than the stage. As I have just said, I expect that the theatre will borrow many devices from the cinema; but I do not see how it can ever achieve such performances of my plays (for instance) as are possible by the cinema. I think the theatre will have to cater for small and select audiences, like the Arts Theatre, the Gate Theatre, and the Stage Society, by doing a class of work not yet popular enough to bear the huge capital expenditures of the film studios.[4]

1. Shaw's responses are to typed questions by Carter.

2. In the 1920s and 1930s, a series of successful farces were produced at the Aldwych Theatre (London).

3. The phrase "four boards and a passion," meaning the minimum requirements of theatre, has been attributed to Lope de Vega Carpio (1562–1635).

4. The Stage Society, the Gate Theatre, and the Arts Theatre were founded in London in 1899, 1925, and 1927 to produce noncommercial drama. Only the last survives.

Arms and the Man on the Screen

(*Malvern Festival Book*, [July] 1932/ST)

Following up the experiment shewn last year at Malvern with the little film of How He Lied to Her Husband, I have this year repeated it on a larger scale with the screening of a full-length comedy. It may interest those who have seen the play on the stage to note how the physical and economic limitations of the theatre are expanded by the possibilities of the picture house. In the play the incident in the battle of Slivnitza, on which the story turns, is not seen: it has to be described in a lady's bedroom. The whole action of the play has to be confined to three scenes, two of them indoors. In the picture the battle is shewn, and the flight of the fugitive whom the heroine shelters.[1] There is no pinning of the characters to one spot: they pass in and out of doors, upstairs and downstairs, into gardens and across mountain country, with a freedom and variety impossible in the room with three walls which, however scene painters may disguise it, is always the same old stage.

As to the economic limitations, British International Pictures have, without thinking twice about it, spent as many pounds on this picture as any manager could afford to spend pence on the plainest and cheapest performance of the play.

Later on, these advantages of the picture house may enable it to supersede the theatre for all except very specialized work. It is in fact already doing so, though the accompanying spread of the taste for and knowledge of dramatic art has reacted favorably on the business done in the old theatres in the old way. But the films, in spite of all their splendors and enchantments, are still in their infancy. When dramatic poets (as they call us authors in Germany) realize the possibilities of the screen, and the performers master its technique, and the great producing corporations, still too much obsessed with the "movie" tradition, can be persuaded that a good play is not ready to be photographed until the actors have grown into it as completely as they do in the theatre after not only a month's rehearsal but a month's performance before the public, then every corner of the country in which a picture house can live will witness performances compared to which this one of Arms and the Man will seem a mere sketch, in which the talent of the actors has produced a few happy moments under difficulties not yet, but presently to be, triumphantly overcome.[2]

1. After the film's initial release to poor reviews and attendance, British International Pictures, without Shaw's knowledge, shortened it so that it could fit the bottom half of a double feature. The British Film Institute has this shortened print. Apparently, the scenes Shaw describes no longer exist.

2. By "'movie' tradition," Shaw means the silent movie tradition, in contrast to a new tradition that talkies might inaugurate.

Witty Shaw "Holds Court" at Hearst Ranch

(C/X/*New York American*, 27 March 1933)[1]

I am extremely anxious to have all of my plays filmed before I die. But the studios arnt yet doing the class of work my plays require. Most of them still think that a play is only a movie with spoken subtitles.

1. Interview by Louella O. Parsons, almost entirely rewritten by Shaw, conducted at William Randolph Hearst's castle in San Simeon, California, where Shaw and his wife, Charlotte (née Charlotte Frances Payne-Townshend, 1857–1933), stayed during the California segment of their around-the-world cruise.

[Hollywood's Immoral Influence]

(X/Speech on NBC radio from the Metropolitan Opera House [New York], 11 April 1933/*TDO*)

An eminent American, whom I will not name, sent me a letter which I received yesterday morning. He said "Do not judge us of the United States by its two play spots, Hollywood and New York."

But you know Hollywood as one of the most immoral places in the world. It is the centre of an abominably [im]moral propaganda. But this is not realized, because the moment you mention, apparently, to an American the word "immoral" he immediately begins to think of ladies' skirts or stockings or something of that kind. He begins to think you are talking of that very admirable thing, sex appeal, the use of which in the theatre and in the cinema is very important, provided it is well done and the sex appeal is really educational, which it can be.

The real thing with which you are corrupting the world is the anarchism of Hollywood. There you put a string of heroes in front of people, and all of them are anarchists; and the one answer to anything annoying or to any breach of the law or to any expression which he considers unmanly is to give the other person a sock on the jaw.

I wonder you dont prosecute the people who produce these continual strings of gentlemen who, when they are not kissing the heroine, are socking the jaw of somebody else. It is a criminal offense to sock a person in the jaw. When will we see a film issuing from Hollywood in which the hero, instead of socking the gentleman in the jaw, does the civilized thing and calls the policeman?

I notice that you have received that coldly. You think, perhaps, that the policeman would bore you. He could never bore you at his very worst, ladies and gentlemen, as those eternal socks in the jaw bore me and bore every civilized person. Try and get rid of them. But, above all, try and get rid of that frightful anarchism that is at the back of it, that notion that every man has got if there is any evil that he suffers in society: that he has the remedy in his own fists.

My own experience leads me to suppose that it is not the heroes or the virtuous people who are good at socking jaws. My observation is that it is exactly the contrary sort of people who do the socking of the jaws, and it is on that account that they are regarded as evil people.

[Great Expectation: *The Devil's Disciple* (I)]

(P/HC to Cecil Lewis, 9 August 1933/DHL)[1]

All right: go ahead. Metro-G.M., which is Hearst, will suit me; but Sam Goldwyn, who would also suit me, is a separate, and I think hostile, affair.

Years ago I began a scenario of The Devil's Disciple, but got no further than the throwing of the tea into Boston harbor, with comic relief of the regatta duck hunt sort, and the unhappy childhood of Dick consoled by the Devil's angel. In fact I think there were 2 angels, a black and a white, as in Marlow[e]'s Faust. As I planned about twenty pictures before Dick was five years old I confidently predict that a screen version will be at least twice as long as the stage performance.

John Barrymore, who was at work in the Metro studios when I visited there in March, would be an ideal Dick.

GBS

1. Shaw wrote from the Malvern Hotel, where he stayed while attending the festival.

[Great Expectation: *The Devil's Disciple* (II)]

(Transcribed letter to John Barrymore, 14 November 1933/CL 4)[1]

I am out of the film world here, being Victorian and very old, and yet too advanced for the poor things. Until lately the film work done here was not as good as at Hollywood. It is better now, and will be better still later on, as it is the English way to do nothing until others have made all the experiments and found the way, and then go ahead with it strongly. And it may be that the development of the movie into the international talkie may operate in favor of the studios which are within easy reach of Paris, Rome, Berlin etc. as against remote Hollywood.

On the whole, I think it is not so much the question of which is the best professional centre as to where you would like to live and have your children educated. And that takes a good deal of consideration. I dare not advise you. The world is in such a mess at present; and our profession is such a desperately precarious one at all times that one can only laugh when one is advised to act prudently.

R.K.O., through Macgowan, has been sounding me on the subject of films for a year past. I suggested The Devil's Disciple as the best selection, provided you could be induced to play Dick Dudgeon. This has just come to a head; and my terms are accepted; but there is one stipulation which I have sprung on them too lately to receive a reply.[2] That is, that Dick must not be represented as being in love with Judith. If you have read the play you will understand that Judith is a sniveling little goody-goody, as pathetically pretty as she pleases, and spoilt and conceited enough to imagine that Dick has faced the gallows for her sake instead of "by the law of his own nature." But the least suggestion that he was prowling after her instead of standing up to her husband would belittle him unbearably and reduce the whole affair to third rate Hollywood sob-stuff. Unless I can knock this into R.K.O. the bargain may fall through; but by the time you receive this you will either have been offered the engagement, which will shew that my stipulation has been accepted, or else the deal is off.

faithfully

G. Bernard Shaw

1. Shaw wrote from Whitehall Court.

2. In 1924, with Eugene O'Neill and scene designer Robert Edmond Jones (1887–1954), Kenneth Macgowan (1888–1963) reorganized and ran the Provincetown Playhouse in New York. In 1932, he joined RKO as producer, and in early 1933, he tried to obtain Shaw's permission to film *The Devil's Disciple* and *Saint Joan*. On 13 November, he cabled Shaw that RKO agreed to Shaw's terms for *The Devil's Disciple* only and script approval by Shaw.

[Great Expectation: *The Devil's Disciple* (III)]

(HC to Kenneth Macgowan, 22 January 1934/CL 4)[1]

—Private—

I am sorry for the delay of the D's D.; but it is inevitable. As you know, the differences between first rate work and shop routine are often microscopic and seem to the routineer to be quite unimportant; but they are just what the first rate man earns his eminence by. I have only glanced through the opening pages of the scenario; but it has been enough to convince me that I must put in about a months work (or leisure) on it before any attempt is made to rehearse or shoot it.[2] I can only hope that when I return to London in May I shall have something to send you on which you can set to work.

I see I shall have to educate Hollywood. It means well; but it doesnt know how to make an effect and leave it alone. It wallows in it fifteen seconds too long, and then starts to explain it. It cant find the spiritual track of a story and keep to it. And it cant tell a story. Ive never yet seen an American film that was intelligible to me all through. And it doesnt know the difference between a call boy and a playwright.

> G. B. S.

1. Shaw wrote from Ayot St. Lawrence.

2. The screenplay is by Lester Cohen (1901–63), American novelist and screenwriter.

[Great Expectation: *The Devil's Disciple* (IV)]

(HL to Kenneth Macgowan, 15 February 1934/CL 4)[1]

I have now read through Mr Lester Cohen's play; and I must tell you at once that the deal is off. I part with R.K.O., I hope, on the friendliest terms; but we are hopeless incompatibles artistically. You will hardly be surprised at this. I am an old and highly skilled and experienced hand in the making of stage effects. They are blundering novices, with the technique of the lecturer and the magic lantern.[2] They are entirely illiterate, and think that eighteenth century English must be changed into Hollywood slipshod to be intelligible.[3] They have no suspicion that even Hollywood slipshod must be speakable and rhythmical before it is any use to an actor. They cannot distinguish between dramatic poetry by a first class author and a paraphrase by the nearest chatterbox. They deal with a famous author for his publicity without the faintest sense of the quality of his work. They put the artistic work—except the photography—into the hands of unskilled fans, and have consequently no technique; only a tradition of blunders which makes the simplest story unintelligible, and wastes miles of film on senseless details which only check the impetus of the drama and distract the spectator. And to make time for these they omit the crucially interesting passages.

Someday they will have to face the difficulty that if they undertake to film a first class play, they must either take it as it is, as they would take the work of any other expert, or else get a first rate author to produce it: a practical impossibility, as first rate authors have their own work to do. It is sometimes possible, however, to find young men—future first classes like Shakespear cobbling up Henry VI—with taste and talent enough to be trusted with the production of fine work. Failing such, there is nothing for it but to assume that the author knows his job, and stand or fall by it. That is, of course, unless the author can stand by and produce his work himself, which is the ideal plan.

I cannot do this: I am too old; and the very few effective years which remain to me must not be squandered in studios. As to revising RKO versions written apparently to shew me how RKO would have done it, I cannot be expected to lend a hand to my own murder. If RKO were to order a picture from, say, Augustus John, I have no doubt that they would have it at once repainted to their taste by a local sign painter; but if they asked Augustus to touch up the sign painter's work and put his name to it he would probably find a better and more congenial use for his time in painting new masterpieces.[4]

When I went into this matter I was dealing with you on the strength of your published work.[5] I do not know why you handed me over to Mr Lester Cohen, who seems to me a very different sort of writer. That RKO thinks him superior to you I can well believe, as they evidently think him very superior to me. They might be right; but his ways are not my ways; and there is no accounting for tastes.[6] I suggest they commission him to write a play of his own to fill the gap left by my withdrawal of The Devil's Disciple, which will either remain unfilmed or go into the hands of a corporation which likes it better than RKO.[7]

I presume you have copies of the scenario and that I need not return the one you sent me. The truth is, I have scrawled it with comments which do more justice to my own feelings than to the work of my fellow-playwright Mr Cohen. . . . [*sic*]

And now I shall begin a new play and forget and forgive.[8] R.K.O. can do the forgetting and I the forgiving.

> sincerely
>
> G. Bernard Shaw

1. Shaw wrote the letter, as he noted above the date, in "mid-Atlantic—outward bound." He and his wife Charlotte had embarked on a world cruise on the *Rangitane*, which arrived in Auckland, New Zealand on 15 March. With this cutting-off of negotiations with RKO (or R.K.O., as he also wrote in this letter), Shaw signed his name more formally than he did on his last letter to Macgowan.

2. After showing a column of British troops on the march, for example, Cohen has characters say that the roads are filled with British troops.

3. For instance, Cohen changes Shaw's "Have they forgotten to save your soul in their anxiety about their own bodies?" (act 1) to "In their haste to save their own necks, have they forgotten about your soul?" For a fuller account of Cohen's screenplay, see *The Collected Screenplays of Bernard Shaw*.

4. John (1878–1961), famous for his bold portraits, painted three of Shaw.

5. Macgowan wrote *The Theatre of Tomorrow* (1921) and, with Robert Edmond Jones, *Continental Stagecraft* (1922).

6. Shaw paraphrases Isa. 55:8: "For my thoughts are not your thoughts, neither are your ways my ways, saith the Lord."

7. Hollywood filmed *The Devil's Disciple* in 1959.

8. The next day he began *The Simpleton of the Unexpected Isles*.

Talkies and Tourists

(C/*Auckland Star* [New Zealand], 2 March 1934)[1]

You must really learn to make your own talkies or you will lose your souls without even getting American ones. The tendency is no worse in New Zealand than elsewhere, not anything like so strong as in British slums and suburbs.

1. Shaw was interviewed at Wanganui, New Zealand, before the boat docked at Auckland. With the correspondence between him and RKO fresh in his mind, Shaw complained, as the interviewer paraphrased him immediately before the quotation, that Hollywood was Americanizing the world.

Mr G. B. Shaw on Film Censorship

(BBC radio talk, 20 January 1935/*PP*)

The Prime Minister is quite right in hinting that, though everyone desires morally wholesome theatres and picture houses, censorships are the very devil. Mr MacDonald did not use these blunt words, but you may take it from me that they represent his meaning precisely. The Archbishop [of Canterbury] speaks of undesirable films. There are no undesirable films. No film studio in the world would spend fifty thousand pounds in making a film unless it was a very desirable film indeed. Possibly not desirable by an archbishop, but certainly desirable by that very large section of the human race who are not archbishops. Still, as archbishops are very like other respectable gentlemen except that they wear gaiters instead of trousers, any film corporation which devoted itself to displeasing archbishops would soon be bankrupt. In short, nobody wants to produce undesirable films.

Therefore, let us stop talking about desirable and undesirable, and consider whether we can weed out from the great mass of desirable films those which are detrimental to public morals. The censorship method, which is that of handing the job over to some frail and erring mortal man, and making him omnipotent on the assumption that his official status will make him infallible and omniscient, is so silly that it has produced the existing agitation, and yet some of the agitators are actually clamoring for more of it. Others are obsessed with sex appeal. Now, sex appeal is a perfectly legitimate element in all the fine arts that deal directly with humanity. To educate and refine it is one of the most sacred functions of the theatre. Its treatment under the censorship is often vulgar; yet I believe that, on balance, the good that has been done by the films in associating sex appeal with beauty and cleanliness, with poetry and music, is incalculable. It is in quite other directions that the pictures are often mischievous; and if a new public inquiry is set on foot people who consider sex as sinful in itself must be excluded from it like other lunatics, and its business be to ascertain whether, on the whole, going to the films makes worse or better citizens of us.

As to the remedy, the most successful one so far has been the licensing of places of public entertainment from year to year by representative local authorities, accessible to complaints from individuals or deputations, and with powers to withdraw licences from ill conducted houses for what are called judicial reasons by a majority vote. The subject is difficult, delicate, and complicated; but so far the licensing has proved the most effective expedient for keeping decent order pending the time when theatres and picture houses will be public institutions under the control of a Ministry of Education and the Fine Arts.

This is my considered opinion, and I am an old hand and know what I am talking about. Sleep on it before you join the outcry.

[The Nationalization of Cinema Created by Talkies]

(X/TL to Augustin Hamon, 13 February 1935/CL 4)[1]

The business is a complicated one.

The invention of the [silent] movie (film muet) was enormously profitable because the audience was the whole world.

The invention of the talkie (film parlant) involves the nationalization of the film and the end of the world audience.

The film corporations are still trying desperately to maintain the old movie system of world rights. Nothing but experience will teach them to face the new situation; for as Benjamin Franklin said "Experience is the costliest way of learning; but it is the only one of which fools are capable."[2]

France is trying to keep the movies alive for her millions of negroes; but this will not last because (a) movies are no longer produced by the manufacturers, and (b) there are negroes enough to make talkies acted and spoken by negroes in their own language (negroes are wonderful actors) reasonably profitable. Pending this development the French talkie has the run of French Africa.

Now for the political side of the question.

All the new States into which the war has broken up Europe are fiercely protectionist. They not only put every difficulty in the way of importing anything that they can produce themselves, but also in the way of exporting rentes [revenues] of any kind. At present many of them have to admit foreign films because they have none of their own manufacture. But this will not last, because nothing is easier than to start a film studio. The old pre-war movie industry reckoned without frontiers. The post-war talkie industry has filled Europe with frontiers which are all the more jealously guarded and strengthened because most of them are in the wrong place.

Worst of all, there is no sign of any relaxation of anti-semitism. Logically it has nothing to do with Fascism. But the human race is imitative rather than logical; and as Fascism spreads anti-semitism spreads. A British subject selling the rights in a French film of his play to an exiled German Jew is behaving very imprudently unless the bargain is one of an outright sale for a big lump sum.

Spain, which includes all South America that is not Portuguese, will soon be in the field with Spanish or Argentine or Chilean films. Until then, English and American films will hold the field. There is not a single French speaking State in South America.

Then there is the general consideration that France is not for me the centre of the universe, as it naturally seems to you. On the whole I should be a richer man today if France had never existed; and you would certainly be in a stronger position if I had never existed. The French bourgeois doesnt like either of us. To make France the centre of operations for any work of mine would be the act of a lunatic on my part.

As to the German film I have at last obtained an assurance that my fees will be sent to me if I employ German firms to manufacture and distribute. I have accordingly got rid of Fox Films and arranged for a new contract.[3]

As Holland has started making films I have a contract in hand with a Dutch firm; and here again I am faced with all the claims outside Holland and the Dutch East Indies that Deutschmeister makes, and have to say No just as I have said it to him.[4] The nationalization of the talkie gives a lot of trouble; but it has the advantage in the case of a failure that the eggs are not all in one basket.[5]

always

G. Bernard Shaw

1. Shaw was at Whitehall Court. As was common practice at the time, Shaw does not capitalize Negroes.

2. Misquotation of *Poor Richard's Almanac* (December 1743): "Experience keeps a dear school, but fools will learn in no other."

3. That year, Erich Engel (1891–1966), who directed the first production of Bertolt Brecht and Kurt Weill's *The Threepenny Opera* (1928), directed a German *Pygmalion* movie. Fox Films, an American firm with branches in Europe, was not interested in single-language rights but in world rights.

4. A Dutch *Pygmalion* movie was made (1937), directed by German-born Ludwig Berger (né Bamburger, 1892–1969). Henry Deutschmeister (1903–69), later head of Franco London Films, apparently wanted to produce a French film version of *Pygmalion*.

5. This proved very advantageous, as the German and Dutch *Pygmalion* films, which were unfaithful to Shaw's screenplay, were not shown in English-speaking countries.

[The Hollywood Method of Filmmaking]

(X/TL to Theresa Helburn, 15 February 1935/CL 4)[1]

I contemplate the popular Hollywood productions in despair. The photography is good, the acting is good, the expenditure is extravagant; but the attempt to tell a story is pitiable: the people expend tons of energy jumping in and out of automobiles, knocking at doors, running up and downstairs, opening and shutting bedroom doors, drawing automatics, being arrested and tried for inexplicable crimes, with intervals of passionate kissing; and all this is amusing in a way; but of what it is all about neither I nor anyone else in the audience has the faintest idea. Scenically, histrionically, photographically, and wastefully, Hollywood is the wonder of the world; but it has no dramatic technique and no literary taste: it will stick a patch of slovenly speakeasy Californian dialect upon a fine passage of English prose without seeing any difference, like a color blind man sticking a patch of Highland tartan on his dress trousers. When it gets a good bit of stuff it takes infinite pains to drag it down to its own level, firmly believing, of course, that it is improving it all the time. So you see it is not very easy for me to deal with Hollywood; and it will probably end (or begin) with European productions of my plays, adapted to the screen by myself.

> faithfully
>
> G. Bernard Shaw

1. Shaw wrote to Helburn (1887–1959), executive director of the Theatre Guild, from Whitehall Court.

[Charlie Chaplin]

(C/SDI/"By Bernard Shaw," *Sunday Chronicle* [Manchester], 7 April 1935)

Charlie Chaplin is the film artist, it seems to me, who knows his job above all the others.

If you analyze the usual films you will find that 75 per cent of the picture is occupied in people getting into motor cars, getting out of motor cars, opening doors, shutting doors, coming down stairs, going up stairs.

The only use Chaplin has of stairs is to fall down them.

Chaplin's difficulty in the "talkies" is not that he is afraid of his voice being heard. He has an excellent voice, and if you met him anywhere you would not know that he is an actor.

But it is obviously going to be no easy affair to find a voice that will express universally what his silence and his gestures have said to most of the peoples of the world.

Chaplin knows this very well. That is why he has been so reluctant to depart from the silent pictures.

G. B. S. on Film-Making

(C/*Daily Telegraph*, 9 December 1935/DHL)[1]

Until I have actually written and produced [i.e., directed] a play for the screen my opinion is worthless. When an author can produce, he is a proper producer. But he has to learn that part of his business. This last remark, by the way, applies to producers who are not authors as well. In my opinion cinema producers have been spoilt by unlimited expenditure. As long as they are not only allowed but encouraged to spend ten thousand pounds on two penn'orth of effect they will never learn to do it out of their own heads instead of out of the company's pockets.

1. Quotation of a 1920 letter in an article by A. C. R. Carter.

Hollywood Pictures Horrible, Says G. B. S.

(C/*Daily Mirror*, 13 February 1936)

They approach me [to] buy the rights of one of my plays, then do anything they want with it.

Later they probably give it to a bellboy to read and he writes the story for the films, taking out anything he wants to and putting in something that doesnt belong.

As long as the American cinema hires bellboys instead of dramatists to write for them, their productions wont be anything but horrible. They dont use dialogue; they just converse in subtitles.

Were I to shew a movie producer how to make a thousand dollar scene for ten cents he'd think me a "cheapskate"; but were I to shew him how to make a ten cent scene for thousands he would say that Shaw was a marvelous fellow.

[The German *Pygmalion* Film]

(X/SH letter to Eberhard K. Klagemann, ca. 1 July 1936/CL 4)[1]

I have to apologize for having left a letter of yours unanswered. The explanation is that it arrived when I was absent from London and has only just come into my hands. I gather from it that you are under the impression that you discarded my scenario in favor of one which followed the original stage version more closely. Now it is true that your scenario writer took the trouble to put in the things I had carefully left out, as well as leaving out several things I carefully put in.[2] But as the great art of storytelling, whether on the stage or on the screen, is to know exactly what to leave out and what to leave in, every one of these breaches of contract was an artistic blunder. If you study the effect of your film at the actual performances you will find that all attempts to drag in matters and people that are mentioned but not shewn in both my scenario and the original play—Doolittle's wife, the lesson in phonetics, the dance at the party, &c. &c.—are failures, and that the successful parts are precisely those with which I had nothing to do, representing Eliza as a violent tomboy, always a popular figure in knockabout farce. I congratulate your librettist on the fun he has got out of this; but there was really no need to put my name to it. When he has learnt that a dramatic surprise, such as the entry of Doolittle, should not be spoilt by telling the audience beforehand that it is going to happen, he may become quite an effective playwright.

        faithfully

      [G. Bernard Shaw]

1. Klagemann (b. 1904) produced the German *Pygmalion* film. Shaw probably wrote this undated shorthand draft of a letter at Whitehall Court.

2. The screenplay was by Heinrich Oberländer and Walter Wassermann.

A Question Too Many for G. B. S.

(C/SDI for Dorothy Royal, *Passing Show*,12 September 1936)

MISS ROYAL: What do you consider, Mr Shaw, is the reason for the decay and almost the certain death of Variety entertainment in this country? Is it due to modern artists being inferior to the old stars of the music hall, like Dan Leno, Marie Lloyd, Victoria Monks, Charles Coburn, Albert Chevalier, and others; or do you consider that the cinema is the cause?[1]

G.B.S.: I see no signs of decay and death. The old music hall, like so many old theatres, has become a picture house; but its artists are not dead: they have gone over to the wireless. This is technically a new job; and they have not half learnt it yet: they still cling to the old appeals to the eye, forgetting that they are now invisible. And they cannot get on without a claque to encourage them with applause and laughter, which shews how weak their minds still are. But there is as much talent as ever; only its possessors must bear in mind that it is useless to redden your nose and pretend to trip on a banana peel when your audience cannot see you.

MISS ROYAL: The early Charlie Chaplin comedy films that made the reputation of that great artist were based on the exaggerated wistful humor of the incidents of the daily lives of common people. Do you think that Chaplin is really greater, when you allow for the capabilities of the films, compared with a twenty minutes turn at a music hall, say, than Dan Leno?

G.B.S.: Dan Leno was a genius in his limited way; but Chaplin is much more than a funny man. He is a dramatist, a scenic inventor, a great pantomimist who has made a world reputation without uttering a word, though his last film let slip the secret that he is a remarkable singer.[2] His personality is tragic; and it is this that gives such an extraordinary intensity to his fun. There is a mind behind his mumming. You should not make these comparisons. They are unfair to poor Dan, who did what he could do superbly.

MISS ROYAL: Mae West and her wisecracks appear to have taken the English-speaking world by storm.[3] Do you consider that she is as great a portrayer of low life as say Jenny Hill, or is her personality as magnetic as Marie Lloyd's?[4] Is Mae West capable of expressing volumes with a wink and a shrug like Marie Lloyd in her songs?

G.B.S.: I have never seen Miss West in what is called a low life part. But do not fall into the common mistake of supposing that Marie Lloyd's charm lay in the winks and shrugs with which she illustrated the appalling doggerel she used to sing. Any of her competitors could wink and shrug and appeal to the popular love of smut as well as or better than she. Her secret, and that of her rival Bessie Bellwood, was an exquisite accuracy of tune and rhythm.[5] You had to dance to the lilt of "Oh, Mister Porter" as she sang it. Ask anyone else to sing it, and see whether any extremity of winking and shrugging will make it go.

MISS ROYAL: Do you consider that there would be a chance for we Variety artists if we abandoned the existing variety halls and devoted our energies and abilities to producing variety films?

G.B.S.: I expect you will have to. But I repeat, the wireless, especially now that television is coming, is your main chance. And audiences of millions of sober respectable people, instead of the old mob of Champagne Charlies, will make you sit up.[6] The music hall artist, even the second and third rate ones, will have to be something of a real artist then.

MISS ROYAL: It is said that variety entertainments are dead, yet how is it that programs are more flourishing than ever and non-stop revues attract vast and paying audiences? What attracts their large and regular patrons? Is it the talent of the performers or the appeal of nearly undressed women?

G.B.S.: Who says that variety entertainments are dead? Evidently people who do not know what they are talking about. But are you not doing a little of that yourself when you talk of the appeal of nearly undressed women? Clothes are the secret of that sort of appeal. In Victorian days, when it was possible to pass a lifetime without catching a glimpse of a woman's ankle, what is now called S.A. [sex appeal] was at its height. Nowadays, when women with less clothes on than Pacific islanders are as common objects as motor buses, Victorian sex appeal is happily dead. The real mistresses of that art are always dressed from their necks to their heels.

MISS ROYAL: Some years ago you refused to have your plays filmed although you were offered huge sums to have them produced as silent pictures. If my memory serves me you said "Films are the rubbish heaps of plays. My plays are immortal." Do you still believe that plays should not be filmed?

G.B.S.: I have no recollection of saying anything of the sort. But, of course, the silent film was no use to me. Back to Methuselah would make a very poor movie. When movies became talkies my turn came. I am keen to have my plays filmed provided it is done in my way, and not by the office boy; but Hollywood and Elstree mostly consider that I do not know my business and that the office boy does. Hence our misunderstandings.

MISS ROYAL: Speaking personally, would you prefer, Mr Shaw, to see the people of this country and America become drama and variety fans as of old, rather than movie fans?

G.B.S.: Speaking personally, I should prefer to see them become Shaw fans.

MISS ROYAL: Finally, do you think that the extension of the movies will eventually extinguish the drama and variety and that in future these arts will only be kept alive by societies of genuine enthusiasts, whilst the majority will only pay to witness talkies?

G.B.S.: Just one question too much. Enough is enough.

1. Dan Leno (né George Galvin, 1860–1904), who excelled in cockney comedy and domestic humor, told long anecdotes about himself and members of his family, interrupted by mutterings and asides. Marie Lloyd (née Matilda Alice Victoria Wood, 1870–1922) employed wittily naughty, but not coarse, humor. Victoria Monks (1884–1927) specialized in songs and dances. Charles (or Charlie) Coburn (né Colin Whitton McCallum, 1852–1945) was best known as a singer, one of whose songs was the renowned "The Man Who Broke the Bank at Monte Carlo" (1890). Albert Chevalier (1861–1923) is best remembered for his coster songs.

2. That year, in *Modern Times*, movie audiences heard Chaplin's voice for the first time in a brief gibberish song.

3. West (1892–1980), buxom star of burlesque, vaudeville, Broadway revues, plays, and films, often wrote or rewrote her material. In 1926, she wrote her first play, *Sex*. She became both a sex symbol and a parody of her image as a sex symbol, whose innuendos, double entendres, and wit are legendary.

4. Hill (1851–96) sang, danced, and did male impersonations.

5. Bellwood (1847–96), a high-spirited singer, indulged in raucous repartee with audience members, usually in the gallery, who got more than they gave.

6. George Leybourne (né Joe Saunders, 1842–84), dressed immaculately as a man-about-town—with monocle, whiskers, and fur collar—sang the joys of dissipation, which he knew at first hand. His sobriquet "Champagne Charlie," derived from his song of that name, was applied to this type of person in real life.

Saint Joan Banned: Film Censorship in the United States

(*New York Times*, 14 September 1936/CPP 6)

Some months ago statements appeared in the Press to the effect that my play, Saint Joan, had been adapted to the cinema by myself, and a syndicate formed for the production of the film version with Miss Elisabeth Bergner in the title part.[1] These statements were duly authorized by me and by Miss Bergner's Press representatives. The facts were as stated; and the way seemed clear before us. The play had held the stage for eleven years throughout the civilized world with such general approval, and especially with such religious encouragement, that the possibility of a conflict with the censorships which now control the film world never occurred to me. Its revival in America by Miss Katharine Cornell has almost taken on the character of a religious mission.[2]

I am, of course, aware that there has been in the United States a genuine revolt against pornography and profanity in the picture theatres by good Catholics who want to enjoy a beautiful art without being disgusted and insulted by exhibitions of silly blackguardism financed by film speculators foolish enough to think that such trash pays. A body called the Hays Organization has taken the matter in hand so vigorously that it now has Hollywood completely terrorized.[3] Without its sanction nothing can be done there in the film business. The section of the screen industry which is out for making money on the assumption that the public is half witted and depraved, has had a thorough scare, which was badly needed.

As I thought that the Hays Organization represented unsectarian American decency I never dreamt that Saint Joan had anything to fear from it. Conceive my amazement when I found that the censorship of the Hays Organization includes that of a body called the Catholic Action, professing, on what authority I know not, to be a Roman Catholic doctrinal censorship.[4]

It may be asked how a Catholic censorship can possibly hurt me, as Saint Joan was hailed by all instructed Catholics as a very unexpected first instalment of justice to the Church from Protestant quarters, and in effect, a vindication of the good faith of the famous trial at Rouen which had been held up to public execration for centuries as an abominable conspiracy by a corrupt and treacherous bishop and a villainous inquisitor to murder an innocent girl. The reply is that I have certainly nothing to fear from Catholics who understand the conditions imposed on history by stage representation and are experts in Catholic history and teaching; but as hardly one percent of Catholics can answer to this description I have everything to fear from any meddling by amateur busybodies who do not know that the work of censorship requires any qualification beyond Catholic baptism. And the Catholic Action turns out to be a body of just such conceited amateurs.

Accordingly, I find myself presented with certain specific requisitions from the Action to be complied with on pain of having all Roman Catholics forbidden to witness an exhibition of my Saint Joan film. What will happen to them if they do, whether excommunication or a mild penance from the confessional, is not specified. On my compliance and submission, and "if the final film appears to be according to the truth of the story, and does not contain anything against the prestige of the Roman Catholic Church, the Catholic Action (Azione Catholica) will declare that the shooting of such a picture has not met with any objections from the Catholic authorities."[5]

The censors of the Action object primarily that I am "a mocking Irishman" (Ireland is now apparently in partibus infidelium [in the lands of the unbelievers]) and that my play is "a satire against Church and State which are made to appear stupid and inept." They follow this up with a heresy which will make the Pope's hair lift the triple crown from his head. In the play it is necessarily explained that the Church must not take life. It could excommunicate Joan and hand her over to the secular arm, but it could not under any circumstances kill her. The Catholic Action is unaware of the existence of any such scruple. It prescribes the following correction. The Bishop must not say "the Church cannot take life." He must say "The Church does not wish death."

At the Rouen trial Joan was spared the customary torture, though she was threatened with it, and actually shewn the rack, where the tormentors were waiting for her. This incident, credited in my play to the mercy of the Church, must, the Catholic Action demands, be omitted from the film, not because it is not true but because it is "essentially damaging." The common use of torture by all tribunals, secular and clerical, in XV century France, must not be revealed to the frequenters of picture palaces. No objection, however, is made to the revelation of the fact that Joan was deliberately burnt alive. The Action would have me teach that the Holy Office was far too humane to use the rack, but had no objection to the use of the stake by the secular arm.

But it is at the crux of the trial that the Action censor gets deepest out of his depth. There is no longer any obscurity on that crux: those who have not French enough to read Quicherat or Champion can read the excellent account by Mr Milton Waldman just published.[6] When the Holy Office cleaned all the childish trifles out of the indictment, there was a perfectly clear issue left: the issue already raised by Wycliffe and Hus which subsequently developed into the issue between the Church and Luther.[7] On this issue Joan convicted herself again and again in spite of the vain efforts of Cauchon and others of her judges to make her understand it. The question on which her fate turned was, would she accept the Church as the inspired interpreter of the will of God instead of setting up her own private judgment against it and claiming that her conduct was a matter between God and herself. In this heresy she was adamant: no threat of torture, no argument, no affectionate appeal to her feelings could move her from it: George Fox himself could not have taken the Quaker position with more heroic obstinacy.[8] The legal consequence was inevitable: there was nothing for it but to excommunicate her and deliver her over to the secular arm to be burnt; for no appeal to the Pope could have saved her: such an appeal must have had the same result as Cauchon's appeal to the University of Paris, which could not understand why he was hesitating.

To the last, Joan, strong in her spiritual experiences and her voices, was sure she knew better than "*les gens de l'Église* [clergymen]," of whom apparently she had much the same opinion as I now have of the Catholic Action's film censors. But when she did at last understand that she would certainly be burnt unless she recanted, she said with her rough commonsense she would sign anything rather than be burnt. And sign she did: her immediate object, apart from the fire, being to escape from the indecent custody of Warwick's soldiers into the custody of the Church under conditions proper to her sex. But as Warwick would not let her go, her judges perforce broke their promise to her. Her voices reproached her for having betrayed them. She recanted her recantation, and thus became a relapsed heretic. As such she was beyond redemption. She had to face the stake and go through with it.

Perhaps as Joan could not make head or tail of the ecclesiastical law, the Action's censors may be excused for being equally at a loss. In desperation they have demanded the excision of all that part of the trial and of the incident of the recantation. This trenchant stroke would convert my account of a perfectly legal trial, in which the accused was, as far as the Church and the Holy Office were concerned, treated with special consideration and meticulous regard for the law, into a judicial murder like nothing except the trial of Faithful in The Pilgrim's Progress.[9] It would restore the Belfast Protestant view of the Church which prevailed in literature until my play exploded it. That is what comes of conferring a power over the drama which would tax the qualifications of a Gregory or a Hildebrand on a body pretending to represent the Vatican without as much knowledge of Catholicism as any village gravedigger.[10]

Besides, the Church was not finally beaten in the matter of Joan. The Church has a place for all types of character, including the ultra-Protestant. It admits that there are certain extraordinary persons to whom direct celestial revelations are vouchsafed. Saint Catherine and Saint Michael, revealing themselves to Joan in the fields at Domrémy, and giving her divine instruction as to her work and destiny, are no more outside the belief of the Church than the Blessed Virgin in the cave at Lourdes revealing herself to Bernadette Soubirous.[11] But just as persons of deep piety can attract to themselves heavenly patrons and counsellors, so equally can diabolically wicked persons, called witches and sorcerers, attract to themselves hellish tempters, personified in the XV century as Satan, Belial, and Behemoth, in heavenly disguises. It was inconceivable to the Rouen tribunal that Joan could be a saint; and the alternative was to condemn her as a witch. That procedure was strictly legal, strictly reasonable, strictly pious. In 1920, however, the Church finally decided that Joan was a saint after all, and canonized her.

This has settled the whole question for the Church. Joan's voices came from heaven, not from hell. And the Rouen judges were not corrupt, unjust, lawless, nor any of the infamous things the Rehabilitation inquiry imputed: they simply mistook a very extraordinary saint for a witch. The Catholic Action must be aware of the fact of the canonization; but it has not yet readjusted its views to the 1920 situation.[12] One of the consequences is that Miss Elisabeth Bergner is to be seen everywhere on the screen as Catherine of Russia, Empress of Freethinkers and Free Lovers, but may not make the world fall in love with a Catholic saint as she did when she created the part of Joan in Protestant Berlin when my play was new.[13]

I cannot accept the pretension of the Catholic Action to represent the Vatican. It has neither the knowledge nor the manners to sustain such a part. It is as obnoxious to the United States Constitution as any of the features of the New Deal forbidden by the Supreme Court.[14] It has no legal authority to enforce its vetoes. Yet it has brought all the Hollywood financiers and corporations to their knees by the threat that if they dare to produce a film banned by it not one of the twenty million Catholics in the United States will be allowed to cross the threshold of any picture house exhibiting it.

But what a paltry understatement of the Catholic position! The United States is not the whole realm of the Catholic Church, nor even as much as half that realm in America. What about South America and Quebec? What about the rest of the world? The Catholic population of the globe is estimated at 324 millions, of whom less than 50 millions are in the dominions of the United States and the British Empire. The Hollywood financiers believe that the Action can by a shake of its head keep twenty millions of Catholics out of the picture theatres. But if their belief is well founded it has but to hold up its finger to keep more than 324 millions of Catholics at home in the evenings.

I am not quite so credulous as the Hollywood financiers. I was impressed in my Irish Protestant infancy with the belief that every Catholic, including especially the Pope, must go to hell as a matter of divine routine. When I was seven years old, Pope Pius IX ruled that I, though a little Protestant, might go to heaven, in spite of my invincible ignorance regarding the Catholic religion, if I behaved myself properly. But I made no reciprocal concession at the time; and no Catholic alive can bluff me into believing that, even had he the Vatican behind him, he could keep Papists (as I used to call them) even out of the saloons and speakeasies, much less out of the much more enjoyable theatres and picture palaces. I will make the Action a present of all the Catholics who never dream of going to a theatre under any circumstances; but I defy it to add a baker's dozen to that number by any interdict it can utter. And I promise it, in the case of Saint Joan, that wherever there is a cultivated Catholic priest who knows my play, he will do everything in his power to deepen the piety of his flock by making them go to see it, and urging them to make converts by inducing Protestants to do the same. Did not one of the princes of the Church in America publicly decorate the first American impersonatress of Saint Joan?[15] I hope this service of mine to the Church may be accepted as a small set-off against the abominable bigotry of my Irish Protestant childhood, which I renounced so vigorously when I grew up to some sort of discretion and decency that I emptied the baby out with the bath, and left myself for a while with no religion at all.

I make all this public because I believe very few inhabitants of the United States, Catholic or Protestant, lay or secular, have the least suspicion that an irresponsible Catholic Society has assumed public control of their artistic recreations. I do not consider public control a bad thing in itself. I greatly prefer it to the irresponsible and sometimes vicious private control which is the real alternative. But I have again to point out that censorship is the wrong method. Whatever its moral and religious pretences may be, it always comes in practice to postulating the desirability of an official with the attributes of a god, and then offering the salary of a minor railway stationmaster plus a fee per play to some erring mortal to deputize for Omniscience. He who is fool enough or needy enough to accept such a post soon finds that except in the plainest cases judgment is impossible. He therefore makes an office list of words that must not be used and subjects that must not be mentioned (usually religion and sex); and though this brings his job within the capacity of an office boy, it also reduces it to absurdity. I find in the copy of my scenario that fell into the hands of the Catholic Action that the word paradise, and an allusion to a halo, are struck out because they are classed as religious. The word damned is cut out apparently because it is profane. The word God is cut out, Saint Denis is cut out, sentences containing the words religion, archbishop, deadly sin, holy, infernal, sacred office, and the like are cut out quite senselessly because they are on the list. Even the word babes is forbidden, presumably as immodest. These absurdities represent, not the wisdom of the Catholic Church but the desperation of a minor official's attempts to reduce that wisdom to an office routine.

There is an epidemic of censorships at present raging through the United States as a protest against the very licentious anarchy which has hitherto prevailed. Through a crowd of amateur regulations and lists of words varying from State to State and even from city to city the anarchists, the pugilists, the pornographers can easily drive a coach and six, as it is useless to check up on the letter if the spirit still eludes. But the serious plays like Saint Joan get stopped because they take the censorships completely out of their depth. Presently the epidemic will abate, and the picture trade pluck up enough courage and public spirit to insist on the control of film morality being made a federal matter, independent of prudes, of parochial busybodies, and doctrinaire enemies of the theatre as such. As to the method of that control there is only one which has proved sensible and practicable. Have your picture houses and theatres licensed from year to year by the local municipal corporation, with power to the corporation to discontinue the license on evidence that the house is ill conducted or for other "judicial reasons." That will put an end to the irresponsibility of the exhibitor without destroying the liberty that is vital in those departments of social activity which are roughly classed as highbrow. And as such departments must be jealously guarded against the simplicity of the lowbrowed (else must we stick in the mud forever) the initiative in prosecutions for sedition, blasphemy, and obscenity should be taken out of the hands of the common informer, and treated as a very delicate and difficult function of the most responsible constitutional department available.

For it must not be forgotten that the alternative to amateur censorships is not complete anarchy but police interference. The censorships are popular with theatrical managers and speculators because their licences act as insurance policies against police prosecution, and keep the agents of the criminal law quiet, without imposing any effective restrictions on the exploitation of vulgar pornography and criminal sensationalism. But as they do interfere very seriously with work of the class to which Saint Joan belongs I must continue to insist on the evil they do, on the good that they fail to do, and on the better ways of achieving their purpose that are readily available.

1. Shaw completed the screenplay of *Saint Joan* on 13 November 1934. Production was to begin in fall 1935, starring Bergner (1897–1986), a Viennese actress who had played the title role in Berlin in 1924 and immigrated to England in 1932, where she became a stage and screen star. Her husband, Paul Czinner (1890–1972), a Hungarian stage and screen producer-director, would direct the *Saint Joan* film. The project came to nothing. *Saint Joan* was not filmed until 1957, seven years after Shaw's death, directed by Viennese-born Otto Preminger (1905–86) from a screenplay by Graham Greene (1904–91), a Catholic novelist, essayist, and screenwriter who de-Protestantized Shaw's play. Neither knew of Shaw's screen version or of the objections Shaw discusses in this article.

2. Cornell (1893–1974), American, starred in and coproduced a revival of *Saint Joan* in New York in March 1936.

3. In 1922, scandals and threats of federal censorship prompted the Motion

Picture Producers and Distributors of America to create a self-censorship agency to improve the American film industry's image by pressuring producers to exclude certain subjects and language. Its efforts were partly effective. In early 1934, Catholic bishops organized the Legion of Decency, which threatened a boycott by American Catholics of "vile and unwholesome pictures." The MPPDA cooperated. With Will H. Hays (1879–1954) as the first president of the MPPDA, it was known as the Hays Office. On 1 July 1934, a new Production Code Administration, headed by Joseph I. Breen (1890–1965), took charge of film censorship, but the name Hays Office remained.

4. While Pius X may have been the first pope to use the name Catholic Action (1905), Pius XI defined it (1922): "the participation of the laity in the apostolate of the Church's hierarchy." Headquartered in Rome, Catholic Action varied in different countries but was organized and performed under a bishop's mandate. Catholic Action was not an official Church body, but the examiners who reported on *Saint Joan* in August 1935 were priests whose viewpoint represented that of the Vatican.

5. Letter from Father M. Barbera, 27 August 1935 (BL 50633). Quotations in the next paragraph are from this letter. For more information on Catholic Action's actions, see the introduction to *The Collected Screenplays of Bernard Shaw*, 53–54. Quotations of prescribed textual alterations are from Catholic Action's marginal comments in Shaw's scenario (BL 50644). Appendix B of Bernard Shaw, *Saint Joan: A Screenplay*, ed. by Bernard F. Dukore (Seattle: University of Washington Press, 1968) contains the proposed deletions and changes.

6. Jules Étienne Joseph Quicherat, *Procès de condamnation et réhabilitation de Jeanne d'Arc*, 5 vols. (Paris: J. Renouard, 1841–49); Pierre Champion, *Procès de condamnation de Jeanne d'Arc*, 2 vols. (Paris: E. Champion 1921); Milton Waldman, *Joan of Arc* (London: Longmans, Green, 1935).

7. John Wycliffe (ca. 1328–84), an English religious reformer who attacked the organization and certain doctrines of the Roman Church, was prohibited from preaching by the pope. Jan Hus (1373–1415), a Bohemian whose preachings urged reforms of the church, was convicted of heresy, excommunicated, and burnt. In *Saint Joan*, Shaw echoes his exclamation "sancta simplicitas," when a peasant threw wood on the pyre on which he was burning.

8. In 1648–50, Fox (1624–91), a magnetic English preacher, founded the

Society of Friends, or Quakers (so called because they were enjoined to tremble at the name of God), who were distinguished by pacifism, plain dress, refusal to take oaths, faith in the inner light of Jesus, and the absence of ministers.

9. *Pilgrim's Progress*, part 1 (1678) by John Bunyan (1628–88), one of Shaw's favorite authors; part 2 appeared in 1684.

10. Gregory the Great (Saint Gregory I, 540–604), an early pope and a prolific writer, strove for the peaceful conversion of the Jews and introduced picture books of the Bible for illiterates. The last words of Hildebrand of Soana (Saint Gregory VII, ca. 1020–85), whom Henry IV of Germany imprisoned after having excommunicated and later absolved him, were, "I have loved justice and hated iniquity: therefore I die in exile."

11. A religious French girl (1844–79) whose vision occurred in 1858.

12. The year Joan was canonized.

13. Bergner played Catherine in her first British film, *Catherine the Great* (1934).

14. The New Deal, as President Franklin Delano Roosevelt (1882–1945) called his efforts to cope with the economic crises of the Great Depression, included aid to the urban and rural unemployed and regulation of banks and the stock market. Among its provisions was Social Security. The Supreme Court struck down certain other provisions as unconstitutional.

15. On 3 March 1924, Gaston Liebert, minister plenipotentiary of France, presented the Gold Medal of Joan of Arc, which was blessed by Archbishop Patrick J. Hayes, to the American actress Winifred Lenihan (1898–1964) for fully representing the saint's spiritual and national qualities in her performance in the Theatre Guild's production of *Saint Joan*.

Shaw Stands Firm on Censor Charge

(C/SDI for Thurston Macauley, *New York Times*, 27 September 1936)

Standing firmly on his original charges, George Bernard Shaw tonight replied to protests following his recent letter to the New York Times denouncing alleged Catholic censorship of the film Saint Joan.[1] He was interviewed in his country home of Ayot St Lawrence.

"I do not have to write for my living nowadays" he said "and should not have dreamed of asking the New York Times for three columns of its leader page if my business had been merely personal business, not United States business.[2]

"The whole thing is a muddle. I am in a muddle still. All I know is that the film business in America is in the grip of a Catholic censorship strong enough to intimidate an English producer into submitting a play for its approval, and its disapproval knocked the whole enterprise on the head although hundreds of thousands of dollars were blamelessly at stake. There is no getting over that hard fact.

"I was stopped but I could not tell exactly what stopped me. I was like a man run over by an automobile without a licence number. I could decipher nothing but the words 'Azione Cattolica,' which I translated as 'Catholic Action.' These 'Actions' have been fashionable in Europe for some years past, but as to who or what they are I know no more than the man in the moon.

"All I could say was that I was run over by one of them with an Italian name. When I raised a hue and cry in the United States I was assured I had not been run over at all and was only trying to advertise myself, that there was no such thing as a Catholic Action; that the Catholic Action censorial arm in the United States was the Catholic Legion of Decency, that Hollywood is not acquainted with me or my work; that Joseph Breen and Will H. Hays had never seen the scenario of Saint Joan and therefore could not have suggested any changes in it; that Mr Breen, who censors screen productions, carried on confidential conversations about the play; that Mr Breen was in Panama and was not expected home til next Tuesday; that several statements which I never made are not true and that all statements I did make were so surprising that they cannot possibly be true.

"If that isnt a muddle, what is?" Mr Shaw paused for breath for the first time. "Muddle is a mild term for my state of mind but, like Father Talbot [the Reverend Francis X. Talbot, editor of the Catholic publication *America*, who said Mr Shaw had 'muddled' the meaning of Catholic

Action], I am beginning to see daylight as the witnesses clear up the facts.[3]

"I never heard of the Catholic Legion of Decency, but what a splendid idea: more power to its elbow. I heard the name Breen, a good Irish Catholic name, but beyond wondering whether he was related to the famous Dan Breen, whose tactics played a part in the struggle for the Irish Free State, I had no idea where Mr Breen came in.[4]

"Mr Hays was equally a mystery to me. I now learn that Mr Breen's job is to give certificates of purity to the Motion Picture Producers and Distributors of America, of which Mr Hays is president. We have had that sort of arrangement in England for years with results that explain the foundation of the Legion of Decency."

Mr Shaw was reminded that Catholic authorities say that the Legion never reads plays or scenarios, that it does not deal with them until they are produced.

"Some Catholic Action or other read the Saint Joan scenario and dealt with it very positively, but the reverend fathers who have urged this point are in the right so far as they know. As they say, their business is simply to declare whether films are fit for decent Catholics to see, and if not, to warn their flocks accordingly.

"But this amounts to telling Hollywood that if an improper or anti-Catholic film—say, Mark Twain's Joan—is produced, 20,000,000 Catholics in the United States will be told by their spiritual directors to boycott it.[5] As Hollywood isnt expert in problems either of propriety or Catholic doctrine, it runs in panic to anyone who professes such expertness for assurance that its scenarios are all right before it ventures $100,000 or so on each. There is always somebody ready to act as a censor in this way for a due consideration."

Mr Shaw was further reminded that Hollywood had nothing to do with his film, that it was an English one.

"True" he replied, "but as English producers look to the American market for an indispensable share of the profits, they are equally under the thumb of the Legion. Thats why Dr Czinner [Dr Paul Czinner, film director] tried to get a certificate from the Vatican to reassure the producers as to the orthodoxy of my play.[6] He was unfortunate in his choice of expert, as my letter shewed. If he had gone to the Pope he would have got his certificate and a blessing for me as well, but Popes have something else to do than read scenarios. A week of such reading would destroy the mind of anyone with a mind to be destroyed."

Mr Shaw was asked what he was going to do about the matter.

"Nothing" he responded. "Havnt I done enough? On the 13th of September last [the day before the letter was published] not one American in 50,000 had the faintest suspicion that the film art for which his country is famous was, in effect, under a Catholic censorship, which was bound as such to operate as a doctrinal censorship as well as a common-decency censorship.[7] Now, thanks to the New York Times, all Presbyterian America knows it. My sole object was to make it known."

He was asked whether he had not proposed a Federal censorship in opposition to the National Council of Freedom from Censorship and the American Civil Liberties Union.

"They tell you so" he retorted. "I never heard of either the council or the union in my life. I understand their reception of my useful and much needed instructions. They have established the dogma of the fallibility of the Pope, for their complaint is that my position is substantially that taken some weeks ago by Pius XI, which I take to be a very high compliment, although it was meant by them as a reductio ad absurdum.[8]

"However, talk about liberty in America is a well known symptom of an incurable delusion. I did not propose a Federal censorship. What I did urge was that the power to prosecute for sedition, blasphemy, or obscenity should be jealously reserved to the appropriate Secretary of State, with the countersign of the President. The Civil Liberties Union prefers to leave it to the local chief of police or the nearest successor to the late Anthony Comstock.[9] Such restriction, combined with the annually renewed municipal licensing of all places of public entertainment, will do all possible or necessary to keep such places in order. Censorship should be entirely discarded. What Hatcher Hughes is dreaming of for the theatre is simply outlawry and anarchy, and thats fortunately impossible."[10]

1. The article is datelined 26 September.

2. The interview did not appear in the (Sunday) *New York Times*'s leader page but in sec. 2, p. 14.

3. Brackets in original.

4. Dan Breen (1894–1969) was an Irish Republican and member of the Dáil (Parliament).

5. Twain listed himself as editor, "Jean François Alden" as author of *Personal Recollections of Joan of Arc by the Sieur Louis de Conte, her page and secretary. Freely translated out of the ancient French . . . from the original unpublished manuscripts* (1896).

6. Brackets in original.

7. Brackets in original.

8. In an encyclical letter dated 29 June 1936 and issued on 2 July, addressed to everyone but especially to archbishops and bishops in the United States, Pope Pius XI appealed for a ban on indecent and morally unsound movies. He suggested that the clergy try to obtain from their congregations, particularly from parents, annual promises not to see offensive films, and he urged each nation to institute a special office that would inform the public by classifying the moral content of motion pictures.

9. Comstock (1844–1915), secretary of the New York Society for the Suppression of Vice, boasted that he brought thousands of criminals to justice and destroyed tons of obscene literature and pictures. In 1905, he persuaded the New York police commissioner to arrest various people connected with the production of *Mrs. Warren's Profession* on the charge of disorderly conduct, thereby closing the play. The court dismissed the case. For activities like Comstock's, Shaw coined the term "Comstockery."

10. Hughes (1881–1945), American author of the Pulitzer Prize-winning play *Hell-Bent for Heaven* (1924) and professor of playwriting at Columbia University, opposed all censorship.

The Art of Talking for the Talkies

(*World Film News*, November 1936/*TDO*)[1]

Just exactly as the change on to the movie screen involved a completely new technique of acting, so that you found the most experienced actors were the most impossible when you wanted to get them on the screen, so the change to the talkie involves a quite new technique. Because of the speech distance in the ordinary theatre the actor has to exaggerate a good deal, both in gesture and in delivery, in order to get to the boy at the back of the gallery. In the intensely illuminated, magnifying film, if they attempted to do with their voices and their gestures what was done in the ordinary theatre, the effect was ridiculous, it was so exaggerated. You had to get a technique of diminution instead of exaggeration. The first lesson you had to learn in the movies was never to move.

Well, that lesson was learnt at last, and then the talkie came along. Precisely the same thing, the same change in technique, came with the talkie. Instead of having to make your voice audible at a great distance; instead of having to remember that certain delicate nuances which you use in conversation were no use in a theatre because they did not get across, you suddenly found yourself speaking into an extraordinarily sensitive instrument, and this instrument magnified your voice and carried it almost anywhere. So again, just as you had to abandon your old exaggerated technique of acting and come back to the opposite of exaggeration, diminished action, so in the same way it had become necessary to speak, to articulate very distinctly for the microphone as you do for the gramophone. You had also to master the rather difficult fact that the microphone, like the gramophone, picks up and makes audible a number of tones and peculiarities in the voice which we do not hear if we are listening to the person speaking. The microphone, for instance, brings out native accents with the most extraordinary vigor, although you may not notice them in ordinary speech.

Some of the Americans have performed extraordinary feats in training American actresses to speak in the English way. I heard only the other day Miss Norma Shearer. I saw her in a film, The Barretts of Wimpole Street, and it was perfectly beautiful to hear the way she spoke English.[2] She almost brought tears to my eyes by the beautiful way in which she pronounced the word "water." I knew perfectly well that her natural way of saying it was "watter," but she had learnt to say it as we do, and that meant she must have taken a great deal of trouble in order to speak in the English way.

But there is more to be done than that. Too often in the talkies we have a cast made up of people who all speak very much at the same pitch and in the same way. If you want to get a really effective performance you ought to be very careful to make your voices vary. When I cast a play I not only bear in mind that I want to have such-and-such a person for one part and such-and-such a personality for another part, but I want to have a soprano, an alto, a tenor, and a bass. A conversation on the stage in which they all speak with the same trick and at the same speed is an extremely disagreeable thing and finally very tiring. You have to select your voices so that they will contrast and you have to bear in mind that your microphone will bring a number of little nuances and changes which, as I say, would be quite impossible on the stage.

We have not thought enough about these things. In spite of the popularity of the film, nobody to whom you talk ever talks about the voices or about wanting better voices, or understands anything about phonetics. Yet the neglect of those things does really make a difference in the money that you get by them. If a film bores people by being a noisy film, a worrying film, people dont know what is wrong but that doesnt alter the fact that they are worried, and come away saying they have not enjoyed it. They cant put their finger on what is the matter.

Now you gentlemen, it is your business to become very critical of films and critical from this point of view. The contrast of voices will make a film very pleasant. As a playwright it concerns me very much. I have always known the difference that it makes to me to get my performance vocally right. And yet I am quite sure it is neglected in the talkies.

[Questions and answers followed the lecture Shaw introduced.]

Q: Is it possible to do justice to Shakespear's verse as verse through the medium of the screen?[3]

G.B.S.: I should go so far as to say that you can do things with the microphone that you cannot do on the ordinary stage. I want again to emphasize the fact that you are dealing with a new instrument and that in speaking on the screen you can employ nuances and delicacies of expression which would be no use spoken by an actor on the ordinary stage in the ordinary way. They might possibly reach the first row of the stalls; they would not get any further.

In all other respects you have to remember, and adapt yourself accordingly, that the microphone is really enabling everybody in the house to hear you quite well and if you have an adequate recording instrument, if your machinery is all right and up to date (which in many picture houses it is not), you must not do it as you do it in Regent's Park.

The main thing that you require nowadays is to get people who understand what they are saying when they are speaking Shakespear. That is really the difficulty, because you must remember that Shakespear's language is to a great extent a dead language. When I was young we were all brought up on the Bible and that enabled us to understand Elizabethan English. But people are no longer all brought up in that way nowadays, and when you are going to a theatre, listening to people speaking Shakespear, try to experiment, as I try so often at rehearsals: shut your eyes. As long as you can see the actor and see his eagle eye fixing the other actor, you dont really listen very clearly and try to understand exactly what is said. But try it with your eyes shut, and especially if he is speaking to some other actor who does understand what he says. The difference comes out at once.

The late Sir Herbert Beerbohm Tree never understood anything in Shakespear except what nobody could possibly help. It was like the schoolboy going through the Latin play or the Greek play. You could always hear the differences if you were on the watch for it.

And I may say that I think the difficulty of avoiding monotony is largely a question of people understanding what they are saying.

You see if people do understand and feel what they are saying they get all sorts of inflexions without thinking about it. Of course if they are only repeating lines they have picked up, not only is the thing monotonous, but it is unintelligible, because they never fix the key word and get it across. You always have to look out for the one word without which the speech is unintelligible.

Q: With the use of the camera you are able to get the spirit of the aside, the soliloquy, much better than you are able to get it on the stage?

G.B.S.: That is very interesting. Because one of the difficulties now is to keep the camera in its place. Often in a studio I have seen an enthusiastic photographer wasting any amount of money and time in order to get a certain little spot of light over the door, which did not matter in the slightest degree, and at the same time a number of actors were having to repeat themselves over and over again until they became lunatics almost. But there it is. It is a very admirable illustration of what can be done. Really the whole business of the screen is a most wonderful art. Nobody I think has yet had the least idea of how much can be done with it. In fact we are at present in the stage when anybody who really knows what can be done with it gets cast out of the studio because he knows nothing about it!

Q: Dont all these devices in themselves constitute an interruption of the verse, the rhythm, the sweep of the verse?

G.B.S.: Well, if they are not used in the proper way, of course they not only spoil the verse but they spoil everything else. It is extraordinary how much can be spoilt if you let the photographer, as photographer pure and simple, get the upper hand. There is the human voice; you have the verse and the lines. They may be deliberately distorted for some reason, but you have to be careful. You have to remember for instance that you are speaking Shakespear, not giving an exhibition of photography.

Q: I think the point really is that if someone was in charge of the elocution in the studio, he would eliminate these errors and would help to strengthen the actors in the performance of their work.

G.B.S.: If you get in an elocutionist you have to be rather careful that he is not too elocutionary. We still unfortunately have remnants left of that terrible old XIX century notion that the whole art of the elocutionist in speaking verse was to conceal the fact that he was speaking verse and run the lines together in such a way that nobody would suspect it was verse. The consequence is that a great deal of it sounds absurd.

If your elocutionist is not up to date and if he is not a fairly all round man, you may have to be just as careful of the elocutionist as of the photographer. It is a great pity of course that the audience cannot throw dead cats, gingerbeer bottles, &c., at the performers. They cannot express their disapproval.

Q: One of the things I think one regrets very frequently is that with so many people the range of voice is limited.

G.B.S.: Of course you must bear in mind that, as a matter of fact, the human voice is very limited and the most terrible things occur sometimes in Shakespear nowadays. You will find an actor, for instance, trying to make a climax. Perhaps he gets as far as one, and the next climax he tries to make on top of that, and then the next. The result is, of course, when you come to such a thing as the last act of Macbeth, that before he is halfway through he is a shrieking lunatic. There you can use the skill of the actor. The actor has always to remember what are his limits. They used to understand this much better. An eminent German actor who was here some time ago was very instructive on that matter. Instead of trying to shout up and up, whenever he made a big effect on the stage he generally went up the stage to do it. He got his tremendous effect, and then, immediately, he dropped his arms and came slowly down the stage, leaving the audience to realize the effect. He usually sat down on the chair, and then he began pianissimo. That was the trick. With the actor in such stuff as, say, the big scenes of Shakespear it is not a matter of voice altogether. He must be continually looking out for the moment when he can get down to nothing in order that he may have some room to get up again. It is part of the trick of Shakespearean acting, that you give the illusion that you are a sort of human volcano, going from one summit to another. These special tricks have got to be learnt for the screen as well as for the theatre.

Q: I dont know why this discussion has become so strongly Shakespearean. The bulk of the speech which we are likely to hear on the screen for many years is going to be of the ordinary people of today. I am all for improving speech; but the speech director must beware of destroying personal characteristics.[4]

G.B.S.: There again we must remember that what you call "natural" speech is no use at all either on the stage or the screen. It is generally quite unintelligible, and one of the things you have to explain when dealing with students. Suppose you have a play with Cockney dialect. They all take a great deal of trouble to imitate Cockney as they hear it, and the result is completely unintelligible. You have to take your Cockney and find out exactly what the sounds are and articulate them in the same artificial way as you would Shakespearean English.

Occasionally you want to reproduce these dialects on the stage, but all the same the people speaking these dialects have to articulate in a way which is perfectly artificial. Then it comes out all right.

One thing I have to warn you about. In good drama I dont think we are going to lose altogether what we call the Shakespearean effect. If anybody imagines that the dialogue in my plays is natural, they are making a fearful mistake. I write exactly like Shakespear and I find if only people will get the rhythm and melody of my speeches, I do not trouble myself as to whether they understand them, so to speak; once they get the rise and fall of them they are all right.

Q: The main function of the screen is to relate the stories in terms of moving images. Strictly speaking, speech should be secondary, whereas on the stage speech is primary. Otherwise the film may tend to become a photographic replica of a stage play. The screen should tend to sever its connexion with the stage.

G.B.S.: I know the tendency in the movies. I once tried to experiment with a little film myself and I was told the thing was quite impossible because the scene remained the same from beginning to end. They told me that unless at every second speech all the characters went, say, to Monte Carlo or some picturesque locality of that sort, it was not fit for the screen. I said "No, I am going to try this experiment. It will be in a single room; and there will be all the movements from the sideboard to the hearthrug, and the hearthrug to the door, and so on. And that is all we can have." Now that you have got the talkie and can have real drama you must not cling to the old dissolving views, the old diorama. You must get rid of it.

It is all very well to say "Now we have got the talk and we are losing the movement." That is not the purpose or point of the drama. When you get the talkie you are in for drama and you must make up your mind to it. You might always have in the same bill—I quite agree you ought to have—your gulls and cliffs and all that. I am very fond of them myself. But you must not mix up the two things. If you want to do a drama, then it must hold the audience as drama. If you say "We must go over to Monte Carlo every few minutes," you have neither decent drama nor decent talkies.

1. VR of introduction to lecture by Dr. F. (?) Esdaile, "The Faults and Merits of Diction as Heard from the Screen," at the MGM private theatre, London, 23 October 1936.

2. Shearer played Elizabeth Barrett in the film version (1934) of the play (1930) by Rudolf Besier (1878–1942).

3. The questioner is Sydney W. Carroll (1877–1958), journalist and stage producer, who in July 1934 presented Shaw's *The Six of Calais* and *Androcles and the Lion* at Regent's Park open-air theatre, London.

4. The speaker has not been identified.

Best of the Year

(C/*World Film News*, January 1937)

Of the seventy-eight films listed I can remember only three: Romeo and Juliet, As You Like It, and La Kermesse Héroïque.[1] The last was by far the most intelligently and artistically handled.

As to Romeo, the conviction of the directors that they knew better than Shakespear how to tell the story resulted in follies and stupidities that would have wrecked any ordinary play with an ordinary cast. Fortunately the play was foolproof, and the cast very strong.

As You Like It was badly cast, barring, of course, Mr Leon Quartermaine's feat of making Jacques bearable and even delightful. It was also badly cut, proving that the play cannot do without Adam and Touchstone. But Elisabeth Bergner's dramatic imagination is so powerful, and her skill so perfect that the moment she dressed as a lad she became a lad. An unfeminine Rosalind is impossible: all the great Rosalinds have been ultra-feminine.

---

1. Shaw was asked to select the best films released in England in 1936. *Romeo and Juliet* (U.S., 1936), directed by George Cukor (1899–1983), stars British stage and screen actor Leslie Howard (1890–1943), Norma Shearer, and John Barrymore. *As You Like It* (Great Britain, 1936), directed by Paul Czinner, stars Elisabeth Bergner and Laurence Olivier, and features Leon Quartermaine (1876–1967). *La kermesse héroïque* (France, 1935, English title *Carnival in Flanders*), the most famous film of Belgian-born director Jacques Feyder (né Jacques Frédérix, 1885–1948), is a comedy, with contemporary implications, about a sixteenth-century Flemish town occupied by Spanish troops. The Nazis banned it after they invaded France.

Films, Plays, and G. B. Shaw

(QI by Terry Ramsaye, *Fame: The Box Office Check-Up*, 1937/TDO)

Why have you such a prejudice against films, Mr Shaw? What is the exact nature of your objection to having your plays put on the screen?

I have no objection on earth to have my plays filmed. There is nothing I should like better than to have all my plays added to the repertory of the picture theatre.

But you have refused every proposal to film them?

No! I have refused offers for the use of my name to attract audiences to demonstrations of how some crude and nameless amateur thinks my plays ought to have been written: but that is not the same thing. Such demonstrations would damage me professionally.

Surely a stage play has to be adapted to the screen by an expert?

Precisely, by an expert! That is why I object to having my plays adapted to the screen by unqualified and unknown bunglers who do not know the A.B.C. of the art of telling a story dramatically.

Would the big producing companies do such a silly thing as that?

Look around you. They never do anything else. They will go to any expense to secure the most skilful camera artists, electricians, painters, scene builders, musicians, and film stars. If the machinery breaks down they do not send for the office boy to repair it: they send for the appropriate expert. But it has not yet occurred to them that drama is a skilled trade.

When anything is needed in that department, for instance when a play of Shakespear's is to be adapted to the screen, they send for the office boy. The office boy, not being Shakespear, takes great pains to spoil Shakespear's work in the conviction he is improving it. The result will be a demonstration of how Shakespear's most popular comedy, in spite of reckless expenditure and first rate casting, can achieve a complete flop on the screen.[1] That is what the office boy would do to my plays. I will not have the office boy on any terms, and that is why they say I object to have my plays filmed.

Do you suggest that every adapter is an "office boy"?

No: it is too often evident that the adapter could not hold down a job as office boy for a week. I perhaps should have said the bell boy. The bell boy's vision of life is a continual arriving in motor cars and going upstairs and disappearing through doors that immediately close and leave life a blank. The film firms have therefore made a rule that ninetyfive percent of a film must consist of going up and down stairs and getting in and out of motor cars. Not even the success of Chaplin has taught them that staircases are not interesting unless the hero falls down them. My plays do not depend on staircases for their interest. I am therefore told that I do not understand the art of the screen.

Arnt the two arts different: the art of the stage and the art of the screen?

Dramatically, not in the least. The resources of the screen are enormously larger than those of the stage. In writing for the screen you can disregard time and space and money to an extent that would make a play impossible on the stage; but the art of employing these larger resources dramatically is the same as that of keeping within the small ones. You have to tell a story and make its characters live and seize and hold and guide the attention exactly as Shakespear or Molière did. If you are not born with this talent you may be the brightest of office boys, smartest of bell boys, or the most desperately hard up of free lance journalists; but if you touch a piece of skilled dramatic work you will spoil it, with the best intentions of course.

Do you suggest that the screen has not a dramatic technique of its own, differing from that of the stage?

I dont suggest. I tell you flatly and violently that there is no difference whatever. The dramatic technique is precisely the same.

The close-up, the fade, the "wipe," the quick changes of scene and distance are all features of the screenplay not possessed by the stage play.[2] Are they not artistic assets if rightly employed?

Of course they are.

Do you suggest they should not be employed in a screen version of one of your plays?

Why not?

Do you expect a studio to keep a playwright of your own calibre to prepare your plays for the screen?

No. They could not find one, to begin with. Any playwright on my own level would be too busy writing his own plays to tinker at mine. The moral of that is that the playwright must prepare his own scenario just as he prepares his own prompt copies for the theatre.

In writing your plays did you not often find yourself limited by the necessities of considering stage presentation?

I am continually limited by the physical conditions of stage presentation, but they dont bother me any more than the physical conditions of my bedroom.

If you had written for the screen in the first instance, would you not have written your plays in a different form?

Yes, of course.

Would not that form have approximated to the form which a skilled adapter would give your plays to the screen?

No: it would have approximated to the form that I myself would give my plays for the screen.

You have written scenarios for films of your plays?

Of course I have, but the result is always the same. They want to send my scenario to the office boy. There is a German film called Pygmalion, by Bernard Shaw. The makers were bound by their contract and their most solemn promises to follow my scenario exactly. They took the most extraordinary pains, and spent huge sums, in altering it out of all recognition. They spoilt every effect, falsified all the characters, put in everything I left out and took out most of what I had put in. They thought they knew better than I. If they had, they would have been Super Shaws. As it was, they were in the position of a yokel who buys a hat for the Coronation in Piccadilly and, finding it not to his taste, brushes it the wrong way, jumps on it half a dozen times, and then proudly walks down the street in it to shew how well he knows what's what in the way of a gentleman's headgear. So now you know why my films are still waiting to be screened.

The Germans may have made a bad adaptation, but does that prove that adaptation—by yourself, if you like—was unnecessary?

No. It only proves that the German screen adapters, not being skilled playwrights, bungled their jobs. Their business was to carry out my screen adaptations, which were very extensive, and not make a spectacle of themselves as silly amateurs.

You are a dramatist, but if you had been a novelist you might have had your books dramatized by another hand. Is there not as much difference between the technique of playwriting and screenwriting, as between novel writing and both?

The techniques are quite different. But you will remember, wont you, that a novelist is a novelist and a dramatist a dramatist! When their work has to be handled in the studio it should be handled by a skilled playwright and not by the cameraman's chauffeur.

1. Possibly *A Midsummer Night's Dream* (1935), directed by Max Reinhardt and William Dieterle (né Wilhelm Dieterle, in Germany, 1893–1972), with an all-star cast including James Cagney as Bottom and Mickey Rooney as Puck.

2. A "wipe" is a transitional effect whereby one scene replaces another, gradually erasing or wiping it off the screen; a wipe's edge line may be straight or jagged, sharp or soft, regular or irregular, horizontal, vertical, or diagonal.

[Hollywood's Customary Methods]

(X/TL to Cecil Lewis, 5 June 1937/CL 4)[1]

Now listen to me. I saw a film at Sidmouth (where we have just spent a month), in which Gary Cooper and Madeline Carroll kept having their photographs taken for an hour or so, much as I have seen a hundred similar exhibitions before.[2] The photographs were very good, and the lighting and scenery first rate. Madeline was very handsome; and the success with which her natural hair was made to look like a dazzlingly shiny wig and flashed at me until I could hardly help screaming to her for

God's sake to take it off, was unforgettable. Fortunately it was relieved by a fascinating series of Chinks and negro train attendants, also beautifully photographed and lighted, and each looking like a whole detective story in himself, with a parallel series of sinister Americans, whom Gary Cooper socked on the jaw from time to time without ascertainable provocation. It was really beautifully done; and it held the audience as a picture book holds a child. The cameramen and the producers had put their hearts and souls into their jobs.

But the interest was entirely pictorial and utterly undramatic. My liking for pictures was gratified to the full: my dramatic side was only exasperated by the splendor of the opportunity for telling a story and the pitiful amateurish bungling of the attempt to do it. I left the theatre without the faintest notion of what it was all about. I could not make out why Gary Cooper socked those innocent and picturesque people on the jaw. As to Madeline, her transitions from being a virtuous heroine to being a crook's decoy were so bewildering that Cooper at last socked h e r on the jaw without affecting in the least her infatuation for him. From time to time they made inarticulate noises with American accents, with all the consonants left out. Not one word could I understand, nor could Charlotte [his wife]. The affair was in effect a movie, not a talkie: a movie without the qualities which the old movies derived from the speechlessness.

Now set your analytical faculty, if you have any, to tabulate all the techniques involved in these extraordinary exhibitions. You have the camera technique, the electric light technique, the face making technique, the costumier's technique, the picture composer's technique, the picture maker's technique (employing builders, architects, and their draughtsmen), and the technique of the stage management. Contemplating this list you will realize the abysmal ignorance of the impostors who talk of the technique of the screen as if it were one thing. Contemplate it further, you will understand how easy it is in the excitement of all these techniques and their triumphs of execution, to overlook the one technique that is not in the list and is nevertheless the technique for which all the others exist, and without which their exercise has no meaning. Omit [Technique] I; and the audience become children turning over the pages of a splendid picture book. Up to a certain point it pays. Most of the studios seem to live by it. But in such studios the dramatist can find no place. They know that they can do without him; and as he upsets them very painfully by insisting on their several magics being made subordinate to his, they despise him, hate him, baffle him, and finally kick him out as a creature who knows nothing about their job.

Nevertheless, they presently want a continuity to set them to work, and a name to flash on the screen beneath the growling lion and the crowing cock.[3] They sent a boy round to Whitehall Court for "the rights" of The Devil's Disciple. If they got them they would make a picture book of the play. The picture book might be a very gorgeous one. Dick would be very handsome; and the close-up of Uncle Titus and Uncle William would suggest all the characters in America's darkest fiction. Judith's eyebrows would be shaved off and replaced by a proper Hollywood pair. Burgoyne surrendering to Gates on the field of Saratoga and marching out proudly with the honors of war, would provide a glorious spectacular finish. All the scenery of New England would be used up in the transformation of my five little scenes into five hundred. Anderson will die at Saratoga and stain an anachronistic Old Glory with his blood, leaving Judith to fall into Dick's arms and make him unhappy for ever after. And nobody at the end would have the faintest notion of what it was all about.

They dont even know, poor devils, that there is such a thing as a dramatic technique.

Now do you begin to understand the matter, and to understand me, and to understand yourself. Get drama and picture making separate in your mind, or you may make ruinous mistakes. . . .

        always

    [G. Bernard Shaw]

Definitely, if you are going to be there, and can put over a front office scenario on Paramount and see it through without interference from ambitious office boys and other amateurs, I will let you rip and be content with a modest ten per cent at a time limit of three years from the date of release. But it must be for the English language only and for the English speaking countries.

    1. Lewis had gone to Hollywood to try to continue his film career. Shaw was at Passfield Corner, a cottage in Surrey that was the home of his friends and Fabian colleagues, the influential thinkers and writers Sidney Webb (1859–1947) and Beatrice Webb (née Beatrice Potter, 1858–1943), Lord and Lady Passfield, who in 1895 founded the London School of Economics and in 1913 the *New Statesman.*

    2. The film was *The General Died at Dawn* (1936), directed by Lewis Milestone (né Lev Milstein, in Russia, 1895–1980), whose most outstanding film was *All Quiet on the Western Front* (1930). The screenplay, his first, was by the newly acclaimed American dramatist Clifford Odets (1906–63), author of *Waiting for Lefty* and *Awake and Sing!* (both 1935). British actress Madeleine Carroll (née Marie-Madeleine Bernadette O'Carroll, 1906–87), whose first name Shaw misspells, was a Hollywood star.

    3. Logos, respectively, of MGM and Pathé Films.

"Not Likely!" Says G. B. Shaw

(C/QI by Arthur Lawson, *Star*, 2 February 1938)[1]

You have been told a string of silly lies. Since Arms and the Man was filmed I have learnt nothing. Neither, unfortunately, have the film corporations.

At the studios the practice is to call in a photographer for photographic work, an electrician for electrical work, a painter to paint the scenes, and an accountant to audit the accounts. But when an author's work is required it is handed to any amateur who happens to be within reach, who botches it as best he can.

That is why in most films the photography is excellent, the lighting masterly, the scenery delightful, and the story so badly told that the audience leaves the theatre without the least notion of what it is all about, but quite satisfied at having seen so many pretty pictures and likenesses of interesting film stars.

Mr Gabriel Pascal, not having learnt How Not To Do It at Hollywood, and not paying his authors for nothing, will produce the author's scenario, and not the notion of the office boy as to how the author should have done his work.[2]

The production of a drama on the screen is a highly skilled art. When this is realized, we shall hear no more of this ignorant twaddle about its being anybody's job except the author.

I am too old and too much occupied otherwise to undertake the direction at Pinewood; but if I visit the studio I shall certainly butt in very vigorously; I should not be welcome there for any other purpose. I shall, therefore, probably take care to stay away. Studio work is hard work, and people who have nothing to do are not wanted there.

1. Lawson's remarks, based on the announcement that *Pygmalion* would be filmed in Britain, included "I am told that: (1) Since *Arms and the Man* was filmed, you have learned that films are not plays photographed. (2) Authors should not butt in—they should leave film producing to film producers. (3) The author of *Pygmalion* will not, in fact, butt in at Pinewood [Studios]. He will courteously visit the place on the first day and thereafter hold his peace. (4) All this is a sign of progress for the author, since he has changed a wrong opinion for a right one."

2. Pascal (né Gabor Lehöl, in Hungary, 1894–1954) was producer of the British *Pygmalion* film.

Bernard Shaw Discusses the Cinema

(C/Interview with Glyn Roberts, *Film Weekly*, 12 February 1938)

I wanted to know how he felt about the new Pygmalion [movie] production, was he pleased?

"Of course I'm pleased, because I've had my own way in preparing the scenario.[1] Thats what I have always insisted on doing if one of my plays is to be filmed.

"People in the film industry insist on interfering with the natural way of telling a story. They want to cut into a sequence which doesnt need breaking up at all, with shots of a California bartender talking and things like that.

"I wont allow that sort of thing. Film producers must understand that the art of telling a story is really a knack which you either have or dont have. Very few people have it. I'm one of them.

"When they want the scene photographed, they get the best cameramen they can find. When they want it recorded, they get an expert technician for that, and so on for every phase of film making except one, the writing of the story.

"For that they get the office boy, or the lift boy, or a van driver. He takes hold of what the expert in story telling has done and pulls it and twists it until there's nothing left of what was originally written.

"There is no essential difference whatsoever in writing for the stage and writing for the screen. Certainly you can do things in a film you cant do in a play; you can jump about in time and place and get certain effects that are impossible or almost impossible on the stage, but the fundamental problem remains the same: you have to tell a story.

"I know how to tell a story, and I know how I want to tell it on stage or screen. No matter how hard he tries, the office boy, who may be a very good office boy, cant tell my story for me the way I want it told: and that is what Hollywood and, I think, most other film producing people always want to do.

"They argue that I am a playwright and dont understand the art of adaptation for the screen. Nonsense! I understand it perfectly well.

"I realize that a screen version of one of my plays may need new lines. But why should the bus driver or the bellhop write those lines? The obvious person is the author of the play: myself.

"Thats what is done in the theatre. As you know, the play as it is finally performed is often quite different from the playwright's original script. He attends rehearsals and sees how his lines work out in actual production. Often they are not satisfactory.

"I remember, for instance, when we were rehearsing my Cæsar and Cleopatra. Forbes-Robertson felt uncomfortable in one scene he had to do. He explained to me that he felt a certain action came on him a little too soon; he felt it wasnt right. So I just wrote off a few extra lines for him to speak, and everything was perfectly all right.

"In the same way, in preparing a film script of one of my plays, the new material should be my own: that is, if any new material is necessary."

The idea has got about that Shaw objects strongly to having his plays filmed. By this time I had got his point of view—mistaken or otherwise—and I was beginning to wonder whether we may not yet see screen versions of several of his most entertaining and provocative plays.

He feels strongly about the whole question of narration in films. He said:

"I have no objection at all to seeing my plays filmed."

"Do you positively w i s h to see them filmed?"

"Yes, yes: I do. Why not? They would make excellent films. I think this one of Pygmalion will really be my Pygmalion, and as you know, Bergner is coming back to do Saint Joan.[2]

"What I have refused in the past is to hand over my plays just for the value of my name and their prestige, and then see them completely distorted by the company concerned. I know all there is to know about telling a story."

He was very emphatic, speaking crisply and persuasively, quite anxiously making his points.

"A good many years ago a little play of mine was made as a film at Elstree."

"That was How He Lied to Her Husband, wasnt it?"

"Yes. It was only a little thing, but it gave Edmund Gwenn some excellent opportunities. Now I stipulated that there should be no changes of scene in the film: no unnecessary jumps away and back again.

"All I wanted was freedom for the characters to move about from the door to the mantelpiece and so on, just as in the play.

"And so it was done. And it was perfectly satisfactory. Audiences liked it, because the dialogue held them.

"That is what I want in film versions of my plays: I want them to be my plays, transferred to the screen with the necessary adaptations and no others. And those adaptations I can do myself because I know how to reach an audience."

From remarks he had made in our earlier talk I gathered that Shaw has no great plans for the future. He is not working on a new play or on a new book. He says there is a liberal education for whoever wants it in what he has already written.

Perhaps the cinema can make use of Shaw's genius at last: make real use of it in a big way. I can well imagine the superior "My Gods!" with which the intelligentsia of the screen will greet some of the theories he has aired in this talk.

But the fact remains that Bernard Shaw c a n tell a story, he does know what grips an audience, and he has a wonderful flair for the clash and interplay of conflicting forces, the very fibre of all drama, whatever its medium.

"How often do you go to the cinema?" I asked him.

"Oh, fairly often—off and on—not quite so much lately, perhaps" he replied smiling.

"Well, for example, how many times have you been in the last year?"

"About twice, I should say. But I go more often when I spend a holiday by the seaside. A year or so ago I stayed in a Devonshire resort for some time and I used to go in every half-week.[3]

"But the cinema is unconvincing; its unreal: and thats because it lacks expert storytellers. Dont suppose that because I dont go twice a week all the year round, as your readers do, I dont know whats wrong. I do know."

1. Of *Pygmalion*, whose first day of shooting was 11 March, just less than a month away.

2. The statement may be somewhat misleading. Although Shaw had withdrawn film rights to *Saint Joan* from Elisabeth Bergner and Paul Czinner, they urged him to reconsider his decision after seeing her act the play on stage. The following summer, on 6 August 1938, she played the first of seven performances of *Saint Joan* at the Malvern Festival. He saw her at a matinee, felt she misrepresented the role, considered her a total failure, and refused to let her play it on the screen.

3. Shaw, who was eighty-one years old, spent most of his time in his home in the village of Ayot St. Lawrence, where he saw films at the local rectory.

[The Ending of *Pygmalion* in the British Film]

(X/TL to Gabriel Pascal, 24 February 1938/CL 4)[1]

I have given my mind to the Pygmalion film seriously, and have no doubt at all as to how to handle the end of it. Anthony is a talented and inventive youth; but he doesnt know the difference between the end of a play and the beginning.[2] Just when the audience has had enough of everything except the ending between Higgins and Eliza, to go back to the dirty mob in Covent Garden and drag back Doolittle after he has been finished and done with would produce a boredom and distraction that would spoil the whole affair. As to taking Higgins and Eliza out of that pretty drawingroom to be shaken up in a car it shews an appalling want of theatre sense and a childish itch for playing with motor cars and forgetting all about the play and the public. So away all that silly stuff goes.

Will you impress on Laurence Irving that the end of the play will depend on him?[3] Not only must the drawingroom be pretty and the landscape, and the river if possible, visible through the windows with the suggestion of a perfect day outside, but the final scene on the embankment of Cheyne Walk must be a really beautiful picture. Its spaciousness must come out when the car is driven off. Irving must eclipse Whistler in this.

I am sorry I have had to stick in the flower shop; but it need not cost more than it is worth and you will save by getting rid of the wedding rubbish. It is not a Bond Street shop but a South Kensington one: half florist's, half greengrocer's and fruiterer's with a fine bunch of property grapes for Freddy to weight for a lady customer. The counters can be made for a few pounds: scales can be hired; and the building can be faked out of any old junk. Everything unsightly can be covered in flowers. . . .

Our advertising line must be an insult to Hollywood all through. An all British film made by British methods without interference by American script writers, no spurious dialogue but every word by the author, a revolution in the presentation of drama on the film. In short, English *über Alles*.[4]

> faithfully
> GBS

1. Shaw was at Whitehall Court.

2. Anthony Asquith, British film director (1902–68), shared directorial credit with Leslie Howard, who played Henry Higgins. Asquith shot three endings and used a romantic one rather than that of Shaw, who makes it clear that Eliza will marry Freddy and that Higgins cheerfully accepts her decision.

3. The grandson of Sir Henry Irving, Laurence (Henry Forster) Irving (1897–1988), English set designer for the stage and art director for the screen, designed Pygmalion.

4. Shaw's paraphrase of *Deutschland über Alles*, the German national anthem, overlooks the fact that the film's producer and prime mover was Hungarian.

[Planning a Successor to *Pygmalion*]

(X/TL to Gabriel Pascal, 1 September 1938/CL 4)[1]

Now is the time to be careful—extraordinarily careful. The success of
the Pygmalion film will set all Hollywood rushing to get a rake-off on the
next Shaw film. Where the carcass is, there will the eagles be gathered.[2]
No American feels safe until he has at least five other Americans raking
him off, most of them contributing nothing except their entirely undesirable company. They get so settled in that way of doing business that they
do not understand how a European with a cast iron monopoly under his
own hat can play his game singlehanded. So again I say be careful, or the
film will make a million and yet leave you with a deficit.

Eli[s]abeth Bergner, though she drew full houses at Malvern, was such
a hopeless failure as Joan that I told her she must drop the film project.
The play is therefore free; but the Californian suggestion of Miss Garbo
for Joan is—well, Californian. If the heroine of the play were the Blessed
Virgin they would probably have suggested Miss Mae West. We must
have Wendy.[3] There is no gratitude in business; and it would be the
height of folly to quarrel with her after we have made her a star of the
first magnitude. Somebody else would get her and exploit the work you
have done with her. She cannot refuse the part, which is unique; and even
if she did, or if she dropped dead, I could produce two young English
provincial Joans who would be better than any Hollywood siren.

As to Cæsar, the difficulty is to find an actor capable of filling the part.
Robert Donat is far too young.[4] The best heavy lead on the English stage
is Trouncer, who played the policeman in Pygmalion, and ought to have
played Higgins. He has just had a tremendous success as Bombardone in
Geneva.[5] The sole objection to him is that he has not Cæsar's beak and
shape of head. But he is our only big gun. His Inquisitor in Joan is first
rate. Cæsar must not be a primo amoroso [romantic leading man].

As to conciliating the Vatican, that is utter nonsense. What Czinner
calls the Vatican (that is how he lost the film) is some petty official who
has a list of words which must not be used by film actors. He objected to

"halo" because it is religious, and to "babies" because it is sexual. I make it an absolute condition that the Catholic Action shall be entirely ignored, and the film made in complete disregard of these understrappers of the Church. Really responsible Catholics will not object to the film; but it is not fair to consult them about it, as it is one thing to welcome a film and quite another to guarantee it as orthodox. When the play is filmed it will be irresistible. The Hollywood simpletons say that none of the twenty million American Catholics will go to see it. When the Catholic Action can keep these Americans out of the saloons and gambling casinos and Ziegfeld Follies I shall believe in its power to keep them away from St Joan.[6] Until then, we go ahead.

Do not approach Monsignor Gonfalonieri; but if you happen to meet him you can explain to him the utterly silly and impossible objections, grossly insulting to me, which were made in America, and say that the play led to great hopes in England among Catholics of my conversion to The Faith.[7] The play practically wiped out the scurrilities of Mark Twain and Andrew Lang which were formerly the stock-in-trade of Protestant writers on the subject.[8] But whatever you do, do not ask him for any official expression of approval. Say that nobody, not even the Pope, could be made answerable for Shaw.

Is it really necessary to trouble Messrs Whitney and Selznick?[9] Why not ask your British bankers to back you on the strength of Pygmalion's succès éclatant [brilliant success]? Failing them there are lunatics in London who, excited by the press notices, will back anything filmable to any amount if it has our names attached. We must shew the Hollywood distributors that we are independent of them as far as capital is concerned. They threaten not to distribute, as they did in the case of Pygmalion; but when it comes to the point they MUST distribute, not only for the immediate profit but because we are insuppressible and they would be unwise to quarrel with us. They will always hope to land us next time, and feel foolish if they are left out this time.

      G. Bernard Shaw

1. The Shaws were at the Impney Hotel, Droitwich, on their way to the Worcester Music Festival.

2. Matt. 24:28. In *Major Barbara*, which was the next Shaw film (1941), Lomax quotes it.

3. Wendy Hiller (later Dame Wendy Hiller, b. 1912), English actress, played Eliza Doolittle in Pascal's *Pygmalion* and the title role in *Major Barbara*.

4. Donat (1905–58) was a British stage and screen actor.

5. Cecil Trouncer (1898–1953), one of Shaw's favorite actors, played the First Constable, who interrupts Eliza and Freddy kissing each other. Shaw's original choice for Higgins was Charles Laughton. *Geneva* opened at the Malvern Festival on 1 August. Bombardone is based on Mussolini.

6. In the Ziegfeld Follies, which began on Broadway in 1907 and ran for twenty-four editions, Florenz Ziegfeld (1867–1932) perfected the opulent American theatrical revue, a combination of musical specialties, comic sketches, and gorgeous women.

7. The Catholic prelate Carlo Confalonieri (1893–1986), whose surname Shaw misspells, was personal secretary to Pope Pius XII (1876–1958) for nineteen years.

8. Among the works of the Scottish writer Andrew Lang (1844–1912) is *The Maid of France* (1908).

9. The financial enterprises of John Hay (Jock) Whitney (1904–82), publisher of the New York Herald Tribune, included films. David O(liver) Selznick (1902–65) was an American film producer.

[Cinema Versus Stage]

(C/X/QI by Roy Nash, *Star*, 6 December 1938)

Does your praise for the film version of Pygmalion mean that you believe that the cinema has now reached the stage when it may be considered of equal importance to the theatre?

The cinema from the very beginning has been of much greater importance than the theatre. Its possibilities are tremendous, though they are as yet perverted by childishly inefficient control.

Spoken Preface to American Film Audiences of *Pygmalion*

(7 December 1938 [American premiere]/*CPP* 4)

Oh, my American friends, how do you do? Now, since Ive got you all here, might I make a little speech? Right! I will. Do you mind if I sit down? I am very old.[1]

Now, its a delightful thing to sit here and to think that although at this moment I'm sitting in London, I can talk in this way to an American audience. Oh—stop a minute—I quite forgot to tell you who I am. I am the author of the film that you are going to see, but I'm also Bernard Shaw: mind you, t h e Bernard Shaw. Your newspapers are so full of me that you must have heard about me. Now youve seen the animal. I hope you like it.

You know, Ive suffered a great deal from America in this matter of motion pictures. For years past youve been trying to teach me how to make a film. And I'm going to shew you really how it should be done.

One thing that youve never dreamt of doing is—when you want to know how to make a film—send for the author. Youll never send for the author. Youll send for an electrician when the light goes wrong. Youll send for a photographic expert when the camera goes wrong. But when the play goes wrong, you send for anybody who happens to be about. Of course, I know its not your fault. Youre not in this business. Well, thats the sort of thing that theyve been giving me in America, and the result is: my plays have not been filmed.

And then the American newspapers say that I dont want to have my plays screened and that Ive always refused to have them made. Ive never refused to have them filmed. I can do a great deal more with them on the screen than I can do on the stage. So dont you believe anything that you hear or read in the newspapers about me and about the film business. I know all about the motion picture business and I'm going to teach you—I mean, of course, the gentlemen who make the films—but I'm going to teach them what really a film should be like.

My friend Mr Gabriel Pascal, who has made this production, has tried the extraordinary experience of putting a play on the screen just as the author wrote it and as he wanted it produced.

If you agree with me when you see this film of mine: if you enjoy it, very well. Youll shew it in the usual way by coming to see it—each of you—about twenty times. And then, if you do that, there will be other films. I'm thinking of doing an American play that I once wrote called The Devil's Disciple. Probably another play of mine, Cæsar and Cleopatra, you may see that on the film. But the really good thing about it is that when youll have seen these on the screen—and if you like them—all the American films will become much more like my films. And that will be a splendid thing for America, and it wont be such a bad thing for me, although, as you know, I'm pretty near the oldest writer here, and I shant have much enjoyment of them.

Youll have to make up your mind that youll lose me presently, and then, Heaven only knows what will become of America. I have to educate all the nations. I have to educate England. Several of the continental nations require a little education, but America most of all. And I shall die before Ive educated America properly. But I'm making a beginning.

Now I think its time for me to get out of the way. I was asked to say something to you. I'm always glad to say something to you. I was asked to say something very agreeable to you. Ive done my best. Thats my aged idea of an agreeable speech. But I'm quite friendly. I think youve always heard that about me; at any rate, it's been written: you ought to.

1. He turned eighty-two on 26 July.

Bernard Shaw Flays Filmdom's "Illiterates"

(QI by Dennison Thornton, *Reynolds News*, 22 January 1939/CPP 4)

Q: If we are to believe what the film producers are always telling us about the low intelligence of the average filmgoer, how do you account for the tremendous success everywhere of Pygmalion, which has been praised as one of the most intelligent films yet made?

SHAW: Only thoughtless people chatter about the low intelligence of the average filmgoer. There is no such person. There are several classes of public entertainment, including several classes of film. And there are several classes of film director, including some who are so illiterate that they cannot conceive anyone being interested in anything but very crudely presented police and divorce court news, and adventures out of boys' journals.

They are usually ranked as infallible authorities on the suitability of scenarios. These gentlemen have never had any use for me and I cannot pretend that I have any use for them.

Q: Do you think that these filmed versions of your plays will bring about a new type of film: films in which problems of conduct and character of importance to the audience are raised and suggestively discussed?[1]

SHAW: I dont think Pygmalion will bring about anything but the confusion of the idiots who maintain that a good play must make a bad film, and that the musical English of a dramatic poet must be converted into the slang of a Californian bartender or it will not be understood in Seattle—where, by the way, they do not speak Californian.

Q: In a note to Pygmalion, you deplored what you called "readymade, happy endings to misfit all stories."[2] Yet you allowed such a readymade happy ending to be substituted in the film version of Pygmalion. Why?

SHAW: I did not. I cannot conceive a less happy ending to the story of Pygmalion than a love affair between the middleaged, middleclass professor, a confirmed old bachelor with a mother fixation, and a flower girl of 18. Nothing of the kind was emphasized in my scenario, where I emphasized the escape of Eliza from the tyranny of Higgins by a quite natural love affair with Freddy.

But I cannot at my age undertake studio work: and about 20 directors seem to have turned up there and spent their time trying to sidetrack me and Mr Gabriel Pascal, who does really know chalk from cheese. They devised a scene to give a lovelorn complexion at the end to Mr Leslie Howard: but it is too inconclusive to be worth making a fuss about.

1. The question paraphrases a passage in "The Technical Novelty in Ibsen's Plays," in the second edition (1913) of Shaw's *The Quintessence of Ibsenism*: "Now an interesting play cannot in the nature of things mean anything but a play in which problems of conduct and character of personal importance to the audience are raised and suggestively discussed."

2. The first paragraph of Shaw's prose afterword to the play, begins: "The rest of the story need not be shewn in action, and indeed, would hardly need telling if our imaginations were not so enfeebled by their lazy dependence on the readymades and reach-me-downs of the ragshop in which Romance keeps its stock of 'happy endings' to misfit all stories."

Bernard Shaw Centenary

(C/QI/*Cine Technician*, September–October 1939)[1]

1: Did Pygmalion lose any of its force in being transferred to the screen?

No.

2: Do you think Hollywood could have made a better version of Pygmalion?

No: Hollywood would have murdered Pygmalion. That is why Hollywood did not get it.

3: Which film version of Pygmalion do you prefer: the earlier Dutch one, or the recent British one? And why?

I prefer my own version, which is substantially that followed by Mr Gabriel Pascal.

4: It has been said that on the screen Pygmalion dates and seems old fashioned. What is your opinion?

Anything that is not the latest ephemeral Californian slang seems old fashioned in that benighted State.[2] I write English—classical, vernacular English.

5: Are you likely to write directly for the screen? If not, why not?

My stuff is as good on the screen as on the stage.

6: What is your opinion of screenwriting as a profession? Is the scenario-writer necessary?

That depends on how much the author leaves undone. The author, if a playwright, should do everything except the shooting script.

7: Would you agree that it is essential for the well being of the British film industry that it should recognize the organizations representing its technicians, and make agreements with them?

Of course it should.

8: Have you seen any films which you think are the equal, from artistic or propagandist reasons, of your own work in the theatre?

What do you mean by "equal"? Nothing, apparently. Pass on.

9: Do you think the British Board of Film Censors is necessary?

It is only a contrivance to enable timid film firms to give themselves certificates of decency. It has licensed some films that have driven me from the theatre by their dull lubricity, and simultaneously banned a film to which it ought to have given a gold medal for distinguished service to public morals.[3] Such certificates are worthless and sometimes mischievous.

10: Do you think the British film industry has any future?

Of course I do. Do you think London Bridge has any future?

11: Now that you have joined your professional organization (The Screenwriters' Association), are you also going to join your appropriate Trade Union in the film industry: the Association of Cine-Technicians?

I am not a cine-technician: I am a playwright.

12: Who in your opinion is the second greatest dramatist in the world?

I do not know; and neither do you. You must wait a few centuries for your answer.

1. From the facsimile reprint in the *Cine Technician*, August 1956, Shaw's centenary. However, the title and headnote erroneously state that Shaw answered the questions on the hundredth anniversary of his birth, (26 July) 1936, which was actually his eightieth birthday, and his handwritten reply is dated 6 August 1939, when he was eighty-three. The British *Pygmalion* film, on which he comments, was made in 1938.

2. Benightedness notwithstanding, Hollywood gave Shaw an Academy Award for the best screenplay of 1938.

3. Elizabeth Baxter's *The Night Patrol*. See "'Film Censorship Must Go' Says G. B. S." and "Mr. Shaw on Film Censorship: 'Efficient for Evil.'"

[New Scenes for the *Major Barbara* Film]

(X/TL to Gabriel Pascal, 21 November 1939/CL 4)[1]

Your notion of a scene representing the conversion of Shirley by Barbara is the very worst I ever heard. Shirley is not converted: the bitterness of his lot is that being an atheist sacked as "too old over forty" he is driven by starvation to beg a crust from the Salvation Army. Get Shirley out of your mind: there is just enough of him in the play. Beware of the temptation to overdo every good effect. Enough is enough: another word and enough becomes too much: the fault of Hollywood.

Besides, such a scene would collide with the Mog Habbijam-Bill Walker scene, and wreck both, besides spoiling Barbara's conversion scene with Bill. Big effects must not be repeated. . . .

I dont believe that links and bridges are needed to connect the acts for filming. The audience will make the jump exactly as they do in the theatre.

I left undone an important bit of Barbara: the words for the Rossini quartet.[2] I have now done them and will send you a fair copy when Blanche types it.[3] It has been a horrid job. Nothing would have been easier than to write a few pretty verses; but to fit them to Rossini's notes and accents, and to provide for the big recurring portamento [glide from one note to another] was the very devil; and the result is queer, but singable. I almost drove my wife mad bellowing it over and over on Sunday night. . . .

     Whoosh!

     GBS

1. Shaw was at Ayot St. Lawrence.

2. Shaw wrote a scene in which the internationally famous Italian conductor Arturo Toscanini (1867–1957) conducts a chorus from the opera *Moses in Egypt* (1818) by Gioacchino Rossini (1792–1868), for which he composed new lyrics. Pascal did not film the scene.

3. Blanche Patch (1879–1966) was Shaw's secretary since 1920.

[Gabriel Pascal's Practices]

(X/TL to Gabriel Pascal, 7 March 1940/SP)[1]

Now as to all these agreements that the distributors want.[2] Well, they cant have them. You say, very truly, that money is nothing to you. So much the better from the artistic point of view, but it throws on me a moral obligation to prevent you from ruining yourself. On every agreement I give you you can raise, say, £50,000 per play. But there is no limit to what you may spend on each play. You are generous and reckless instead of having, as you need to have in this business, a heart like the nether millstone. And you have mad fancies for introducing Chinamen, in colors which you cannot photograph, into all-British films.[3] If I give you contracts for nine plays you will raise £450,000 on them, and spend it all on a single Chinaman. Then, having nothing left for the other films, you will have to borrow at 50% from hysterical serpents and others who will bleed you white. I shall get nothing; and you will get worse than nothing: that is, ruin, bankruptcy, disgrace, despair, and suicide.

Now there is only one way in which I can make you set a limit to your expenditure on each play; and that is to give you one agreement at a time. It is no use telling me that United Artists must have their announcements ready three years ahead. They may also want the moon and the stars. The reply is that they cant have them.

When Barbara is finished it will be time enough to think of her successor.

GBS

1. Shaw was at Whitehall Court.

2. American distributors, who were reluctant to conclude one-picture deals, wanted Pascal, who directed and produced *Major Barbara*, to secure Shaw's agreement to film other plays. *Barbara* was filmed during the Battle of Britain. Bombs near and on the studio and in London, plus other wartime conditions, combined with Pascal's reckless extravagance to cause delays in the film, which went over budget and beyond its shooting schedule.

3. Pascal cast the Chinese dramatist S(hi-i) I. Hsiung (b. 1902) as a laundryman in one of the Salvation Army scenes. *Major Barbara* was filmed in black and white.

[Returning Bill Walker at the End of *Major Barbara*]

(TL to Gabriel Pascal, 28 July 1940/*SP*)[1]

It is not possible to bring back Bill unless you are prepared for his marrying Barbara and becoming the hero of the play in place of Cusins. He is finished and done with in the second act. To drag him back merely to give the actor another turn because he is so good is one of those weaknesses which an author must resist: to bring an actor on the stage with nothing to do after he has made his effect in scenes where he was all important is to spoil his part and make a disappointment of him instead of a success.[2]

I say nothing about the impossibility of his becoming a model citizen with a new suit of clothes in a single night: audiences accept such impossibilities, as they do in the case of Shirley.

What you really miss is a more complete reassurance of Barbara as to the loss of Bill's soul. But the only way to mend that is by enlarging Undershaft's speech to her before they go to the factory when she reproaches him with having turned her convert into a wolf, like this:

"Did he not spit in Todger's eye to save his honor? Did he not give up his hard earned pound to save his soul? Do you not know what a pound means to such a man?: more than ten thousand pounds to me! Will he ever strike a woman again as he struck Jenny Hill? It is your faith that is failing, not his. You have set him on the road to his salvation: it may not be your road; but he will not turn back. You have finished with Bill: your work is done in the Army. So put on your hat and come and have a look at m y work."

You can put that patch into the reel if you like: it will give Barbara a better cue for recovering her joyousness; but that is all that can be done.[3]

You know I would change the last act if I could; but it will not work.

My apologies for interfering on Friday. I tried to keep quiet; but I suddenly felt 20 years younger, and couldnt.[4]

GBS

1. Shaw was back at Ayot St. Lawrence. He wrote new scenes for *Major Barbara* while Pascal filmed it. Pascal proposed a new scene at the end in which Bill Walker, given a job by Undershaft, becomes a changed man. Shaw rejected this idea, but at one point he grudgingly relented. Pascal filmed it, recycling a few phrases used earlier. By the time Shaw reobjected, it was too late to change the ending.

2. As Bill Walker, Robert Newton (1905–65), British character actor, was a big hit.

3. He followed Shaw's suggestion.

4. Friday was Shaw's birthday, 26 July. That day he went to Albert Hall, where Pascal shot the large Salvation Army meeting, and was an enthusiastic extra in the large crowd.

[Revising *Major Barbara* for the Screen]

(TL to Gabriel Pascal, 25 September 1940/SP)[1]

You must cut out the entrance of Shirley, who can reappear without any explanation when he is wanted later. The sequence will then read

UNDERSHAFT. No; but I can buy the Salvation Army.

CUSINS. Tell that to Barbara if you dare. Here she is.

BARBARA. We have just had a splendid experience meeting etc etc.

The alternative is to restore the omitted 18 speeches between the two men ending with

UNDERSHAFT. And not on Trade Unionism and Socialism. Excellent.

CUSINS. Bah! You are only a profiteer after all.

UNDERSHAFT. And this is an honest man.

This retains Shirley's entrance; but I recommend the first version, as it will be much easier, and the omitted altercation, though effective as a climax, is much more stagey than screeny and not worth the trouble.[2]

In haste

G. Bernard Shaw

1. Shaw was still at Ayot St. Lawrence. Because Cusins's "You really are an infernal old rascal" was cut, Pascal needed a line to follow Undershaft's "No; but I can buy the Salvation Army."

2. Pascal accepted Shaw's recommendation.

[Promoting *Major Barbara* in America]

(P/X/TL to Marjorie Deans, 25 January 1941/DHL)[1]

Tell all these people, with the utmost possible hauteur, that a Pascal-Shaw film either succeeds or fails: the silly little tricks by which they push their ordinary trash on to the exhibitors have no place in our business. I send no messages and make no appearances at trade shows: I remain majestically aloof, a Mahatma in the mountains of Thibet. . . .

Faithfully,

G. Bernard Shaw

P.S. Please tell Gabriel not to waste a moment of his precious time on this trade rubbish about messages and the like. They will not make a penny difference to us. We either succeed colossally or flop; and nothing wc can do when the film is finished can affect that alternative by a farthing. The tricks of the trade cannot help us; but the tricksters like to pretend that it is they who have made the success and therefore try to get in their repertory every time. He must tell them all to go to ———.[2]

1. Shaw was at Ayot St. Lawrence. The text is from a typed copy of the letter. Deans (1901–82) worked closely with Gabriel Pascal on the films *Major Barbara* (1941) and *Caesar and Cleopatra* (1945) as his scenario editor and general assistant.

2. Dashes (for "hell") are in the typed copy of the letter.

The R.A.D.A. Graduates' Keepsake & Counsellor[1]

(X/May 1941/*TDO*)

In film work the extent to which the time and endurance of the players may be wasted through want of organization is so great that players must defend themselves vigorously through their professional association. No trade unionist workman will do a stroke of work that is not part of his particular technical job, nor tolerate such a proceeding on the part of a fellow worker; but a player may be called on to repeat a scene over and over until the words have lost all meaning to enable the producer and cameraman to arrive by trial and error at the exact lighting they desire. The rebellion of the stars against this has produced the stand-in substitute; but much more could be done in this and other ways to relieve the players from mechanical drudgeries that spoil their artistic work and in any case are as foreign to their specific art as scene shifting or theatre cleaning. But such abuses cannot be remedied by individual complaints and "making scenes" at rehearsals. The electrician will not do the work of the scene shifter; but both would be helpless slaves without their trade unions; and the players must realize that unless and until they have a strong professional organization, providing for its funds and obeying its rules, they, too, will be slaves in the hands of their employers and directors.

1. Shaw wrote an unsigned introduction to this Keepsake; obtained and edited "advice" from twelve notable actors, producers, and friends of the theatre; and underwrote its printing costs. For some twenty years, it was presented to graduates of the Royal Academy of Dramatic Art.

[Taxation Problems (I)]

(SH to C. Walter Smee, 9 August 1941 /CL 4)[1]

Pascal starts for America next Monday, the 10th inst. I can explain the situation less volcanically.

I do not know what are the legal implications of the word Evasion; but I presume that any man in business may legitimately shut up his shop if he cannot keep it open without sacrifices which he cannot afford, and wait to reopen it until the market considerations are more favorable. My business as a playwright is the licensing of performances and film exhibitions in consideration of royalties on the receipts. If I suspend the issue of licences until the market recovers I take it that I am within my rights, and that you may abet me without being disqualified as an accountant or shot as a traitor, notwithstanding that we wilfully prevent a flow of dollars to this country which the Treasury wishes to secure.

The Pygmalion film brought me in the first year £25,000, being 10% on the money paid by the exhibitors to the distributors. Therefore the proceeds must have considerably exceeded £250,000, of which, after deducting the American distributors commission of say, 25% (they are glad to take 17½% now that Shaw is ranked as a gold mine), enough came to this country from America to make the Treasury very keen on our going ahead. The Canadian Government and the Royal Bank of Canada are equally keen.

But the receipt of £25,000 in one year has ruined me by putting me into the class which is allowed to retain only sixpence of every pound it receives. My 25,000 sixpences did not pay the rent of my flat in White-hall.[2] Pascal is similarly ruined. The Treasury and Canadian Government now ask us to produce four new films in the next two years: Arms and the Man, Saint Joan, Captain Brassbound's Conversion, and The Devil's Disciple. I reply that I cannot afford to. They may argue that it is my duty to the country to consent, as I am no worse off than other rich citizens; but this does not apply, as I do not possess an income of £25,000 a year which will persist after the war, but am gambling on a windfall that may not materialize; for any film may flop and thereby be made worthless for the rest of my life. Authors should be allowed to average their income for 20 years for taxation purposes. The other day an author took the Inland Revenue into court on the question of whether his copyright, which he had sold, was not capital and therefore exempt from taxation as such. But the court decided against him. I must therefore either go out of business for the duration or else devise some arrangement whereby I may legitimately defer coming into taxable possession of any royalties on the said four plays until the national expenditure falls below its present level of 12 millions a day. Meanwhile I can live on my capital and on my normal earnings.

Instead of the usual 5 years contract by which the producers are bound to pay me 10% of the money paid by the exhibitors to the distributors month by month I want the following conditions. The first charge on these receipts to be the formation of a reserve fund of the 20% deposited in the Royal Bank of Canada to secure the fees of the author and director. This charge to have priority of all other private liabilities, and the director's half share (10%) to be prior to the author's. This reserve fund must be in the nature of a trust for the benefit of G. B. S. and G. P.; but it must not stand in their names or confer taxable posses- sion on them until they demand it or some part of it from Pascal Films Ltd. and are duly paid by that firm.

An alternative plan would be a formation of a limited Liability Com- pany by G. B. S., G. P., and the British or Canadian Government or the bank, its capital assets being 4 licences, G. P.'s services as director, and money advanced by the Government or the bank or by private specula- tors, the dividends of G. B. S. and G. P. to be limited to 10% each, and their shares classed as preference shares.

Again alternatively, if I sold my interest in the four copyrights for five years for promissory notes for £25,000 each, payable five years from the dates of release of the films, would the notes be taxable as securities in my possession? Can an unliquidated security be taxed?

These are all the expedients I can think of at present. Whatever the solution arrived at it will be stipulated that [of] all the dollars earned by the films in America 50% shall be offered for sale to the Treasury here.

If when you have recovered from the perusal of this letter you have any advice to give me, I shall appreciate it. But Pascal has his New York Solicitor, who is also my solicitor, at work on the problem; and I am sending a copy to him accordingly.[3]

> faithfully
> G. Bernard Shaw

1. Shaw was at Ayot St. Lawrence. Smee (b. 1890), a chartered accountant, was with the London firm F. Rowland & Co.
2. 10 Adelphi Terrace is in the Whitehall area of London.
3. Benjamin Stern was the solicitor.

[On Gabriel Pascal]

(C/*Family Circle* [New York], 19 September 1941)[1]

Gabriel Pascal is one of those extraordinary men who turn up occasionally—say once in a century—and may be called godsends in the arts to which they are devoted. Pascal is doing for the films what Diaghileff did for the Russian Ballet.[2] Until he descended on me out of the clouds I could find nobody who wanted to do anything with my plays on the screen but mutilate them, murder them, give their cadavers to the nearest scrivener without a notion of how to tell the simplest story in dramatic action and instructed that there must be a new picture every ten seconds and that the duration of the whole feature must be 45 minutes at the extreme outside. The result was to be presented to the public with my name attached and the assurance that nobody need fear that it had any Shavian quality whatever, and was not real genuine Hollywood. Under such condition I of course would not let my plays be filmed at all, though I quite realized their possibilities in that medium.

When Gabriel appeared out of the blue I just looked at him and handed him Pygmalion to experiment with. His studio was immediately infested with script writers, and he thought that everything they did was wrong and that everything I did was right. Naturally I quite agreed with him. Pygmalion was an enormous success. When he tackled Barbara there was not a script writer left in the studio, and when he wanted a new "sequence," he very simply asked me for it and got it. He shocks me by his utter indifference to the cost; but the result justifies him; and Hollywood, which always values a director in proportion to the money he throws away, is now at his feet; for he throws it away like water.

The man is a genius: that is all I have to say about him.

G. Bernard Shaw

1. Letter to Stewart Robertson, 12 July 1941, intended for publication. The journal does not cite Shaw's address, but he was probably at Ayot St. Lawrence.

2. Sergey Pavlovich Diaghileff or Diaghilev (1872–1929), Russian impresario, first presented his Ballet Russes in Paris in 1909 and brought the company to London in 1911. They were internationally influential.

[Revising *Arms and the Man* for Hollywood (I)]

(P/HC to Marjorie Deans, 13 October 1941/DHL)[1]

I shall write nothing more for Arms. It is a comedy, rapid and compact, the opposite of Barbara. In a comedy you can be discursive in the first act; but the pace and the closeness of the action must quicken and concentrate after the principal situation until it is going all out at the end.

The notion of developing Louka and giving her funny scenes with Nicola is ruinous. Not another word must be given to them; and they are both serious characters without a touch of comedy. Neither must be played by comedians. All the fun is for the Petkoff family; and Gabriel must give all his attention to Raina, who must be a consummate comedian acting for all she is worth all the time. The tragic parts, Sergius, Louka, Nicola, play themselves. If Ginger is to be the star she must play Raina.[2]

As to the Disciple, not during the war.[3] It is anti-British, and must wait.

G. B. S.

1. Shaw was at Ayot St. Lawrence.

2. Pascal was negotiating with RKO to remake *Arms and the Man* starring Ginger Rogers, who wanted Shaw to rewrite it so that Louka, not Raina, would be the star role.

3. Pascal was also negotiating for a Hollywood film version of *The Devil's Disciple*.

[Revising *Arms and the Man* for Hollywood (II)]

(TL to Gabriel Pascal, 20 October 1941/*SP*)[1]

Marjorie has been pressing me to change Arms and the Man into
The Chocolate Soldier, with Louka written up as the star part with a
dance and plenty of laughs for Miss Rogers. That would suit Hollywood
to perfection: they love The Chocolate Soldier there, and have not the
faintest notion of serious comedy. Marjorie insists that this is what you
want; and she evidently quite agrees with you, and thinks I am an
obsolete old relic of days before cinemas were invented.

Now read attentively. Arms is a play for four comedians, two of front
rank, Raina and Bluntschli, both juveniles, and two elderly ones with
well worn parts suited to their age. These four make all the fun and get
all the laughs. They must be real actors: their parts will not play themselves. On them the play depends.

As a background to throw them into comic relief and give dignity to
the play there is a secondary group who are striking and tragic, never
funny though they are in scenes which are funny, with parts that play
themselves if they are properly cast and professionally competent. They
are Sergius, Louka, and Nicola. They function as a dark background;
and must not for a moment intrude on the function of the comic four. If
Nicola were played by a low comedian; if Louka uttered a single joke or
danced a single step; if Sergius ceased for a moment to be Byronically
tragic and sardonic, the play would be ruined at once, and would drop
to the level of The Chocolate Soldier, in which all the men are cads,
cowards or vieux marcheurs [old rakes] and all the women amateur
whores; and Gabriel Pascal would sink into the common ruck of
Hollywood hack producers.

Tell Miss Rogers that Raina is the star part, and if she is to be the
star she must play it. If not she goes out of the cast; for it would do her
no good professionally to play a part secondary to that of the star. If she
suggests that the part of Louka might be made the star part by giving her
more to say and introducing a dance for her, do not argue with her: just
throw her out of the window and tell her not to come back.

Do not change the scene in the last act. Once the play gets hold of the audience, it no longer wants changes and interruptions; the play must concentrate and accelerate towards the end. You can do fifty things in the first act that would be intolerable in the last. Petkoff's library has a big window shewing the landscape. Changes from that to the stove or opposite corner, or from the ottoman to the kitchen table will give you all the variety you need.

I have seen the first act played as a melodrama with Bluntschli as a sympathetic hero and Raina as a tender innocent heroine taking all her operatic affectations quite seriously: the effect was unbearable. Such a misunderstanding is possible; so look out for it and crush it at the start.

Take care to secure a serious actor for Nicola: a funny man would upset everything.

Bluntschli must speak crisply and matter-of-factly and never declaim: Sergius always declaims.

Marjorie says Olivier will play Sergius. Will Vivien play Louka?[2] I should not advise her to; but if she does not object you need not. But Raina must be the leading part no matter who plays Louka, though Louka may play as strongly as she likes on the lines of the part. Wendy could play Louka; but so could lots of other actresses. The only question therefore is whether her previous association with our two successes is not worth keeping up. I think it is; but then I have not to deal with her personally; and you have.

Everyone in Hollywood will give you the wrong advice about this, because the technique of high comedy is quite beyond them. But you are in a supremely strong position at the moment and need not conciliate their folly in any way. You will never be in as strong a position again, though you may be a much richer man. There will be a rush of producers to imitate you by putting wellknown plays on the screen unaltered. Most of them will make a mess of it; but some of them will succeed; and when this happens you will have competitors. You have none at present, though one film magnate is pressing me hard and swearing that he always does what you do. So make the most of your supremacy while it lasts; and tell all the important people, whether they are stars or financiers, that you are the star this time, and that what you say goes. I took this line strongly with General Films here through the National Provincial Bank when they refused to settle your bills; and they immediately coughed up £3000. Nevertheless they are still frightened by the cost of Major Barbara; so be as economical as your nature permits. They are divided between their fear of losing their money, and their tendency to think you as great as the sums you cost them.

Stern's letter of the 27th Sept has reached me. I was quite prepared for the breakdown of the Canadian plan; but I was surprised at being told that your United Artists contract was "onerous," and that I had complained of it as unfair. That is not my recollection of the affair. I understood that it was the Metro contract that was onerous, and that the U.A. one was a great improvement on it. However, if R.K.O. is better and safer it doesnt matter. The letter is satisfactory as far as it goes or can go until the documents are agreed and executed. The celerity with which you find a new plan of campaign when the old one breaks down is very reassuring.

I take it that Brassbound is to follow Arms.[3] I forgot to say that the part of Katharine in Arms does not need a star with a temperament and a huge salary. (It is a mistake to give a big noise a part not good enough for her merely to get her name into the bill. It inevitably produces a disappointment; and disappointments are the very devil: they spread over the whole performance. Much better give a good part to a nobody who can make a surprising success of it.) She would not only not be worth her cost in money but would upset the balance of the play, which is extremely delicate in comedy, though in big stuff like Major Barbara or Methuselah it would not matter.

Take care of yourself, and do not rush into too many sidetracks and burn the candle at both ends. R.K.O. should insure your life heavily. That would replace their money if you started again in another world; but I could not replace you. So be good.

always yours

G. Bernard Shaw

1. Shaw was still at Ayot St. Lawrence.

2. Vivien Leigh, who was married to Laurence Olivier, would play the female lead in Pascal's next film, *Caesar and Cleopatra*. Olivier would play General Burgoyne in the movie version of *The Devil's Disciple*.

3. *Captain Brassbound's Conversion*. This play has not yet been filmed.

G. B. S. Tells "Why My Play Goes to Hollywood"

(C/QI by Ernest Betts, *Sunday Express*, 9 November 1941)[1]

American papers say that Arms and the Man is to be made in Hollywood by Gabriel Pascal with Ginger Rogers in the part of Raina. Is this information correct and has the plan your approval?

Yes, so far. But in the film world no plan can be depended on for more than five minutes.

Plays of yours so far produced have all been as films in this country. Will you allow any of them to be made in America?

They must be made where they can. If possible my films will be British films. But for the moment they must be made in Hollywood because the plant and equipment are there. We tried hard to have studios built in Canada; but we could get no steel and no labor: it was all needed to deal with Mr Hitler. And he was making the English studios impossible. He nearly wrecked Major Barbara at Denham.

Are you, as reported, writing a play direct for the screen?

No. I am not writing a play at present. A playwright who writes nothing but plays soon gets played out. Are you aware that Richard Wagner's books about political philosophy are more numerous than his musical scores?

Should plays be adapted to the screen from stage versions?

All plays that are any good will have to be adapted to the screen. And already more plays are written for the screen than for the stage. The difference is that 250 times as much money can be spent on the production of a play for the screen as for the stage. Dramatic poets are not likely to let that enormous advance in performing possibilities go for nothing. The art is exactly the same.

Have you any advances in film technique for forthcoming plays of yours?

No. I can work to any technique: so can any real playwright. No doubt advances will be made; but I do not bother about them: I write for the existing technique, not for the imaginary ones of the future.

1. This QI has been collated with the original at the Everett Needham Case Library, Colgate University, with questions typed by Ernest Betts and handwritten responses by Shaw.

[Taxation Problems (II)]

(TL to D. Kilham Roberts, 17 September 1942/CL 4)[1]

A point of enormous importance to authors has been raised by the war taxation. My royalty on the Pygmalion film brought me in over £20,000 in the first year, and thereby subjected me to income and surtax at the rate of 19/6d in the pound not only on those royalties but on my entire income, plus my wife's. Within the two years affected by this apparent windfall, I had to pay £50,000 to the Exchequer because of my supposed good fortune. Another such stroke of luck would ruin me. The royalties due to me from the Barbara film must also exceed £20,000; but I have refused to touch them until all production expenses, amounting to £235,000, are paid off. I am doing all I can to prevent anyone paying me anything lest I should be utterly ruined.

In short, the author who has a windfall of £20,000 plus one farthing once in 86 years is taxed at the same rate as the plutocrat who enjoys a settled income of over £20,000 a year from the cradle to the grave.

Now comes the purpose of this letter. An accountant assures me that an author's rights are his capital. Consequently if he sells his rights outright or for a fixed period, the price he receives is not taxable as income any more than the price obtained by a sale of stocks. If I had sold my Pygmalion rights for £30,000, I should not have been taxed on that sum.

What is the legal position of this?[2] What is the practice (Emlyn

Williams and others are reported to have sold film rights for lump sums)?[3] The Society, if it has not ascertained this[,] should obviously do so, taking counsel's opinion if necessary. Members are entitled to an answer.

To bring the matter to a head, I, as a member, demand an answer.

Perhaps you have gone into it and can answer straight off. I have an offer on hand which depends on it.

faithfully

G. Bernard Shaw

1. After G. Herbert Thring retired in 1930, D(enis) Kilham Roberts (1903–76), a barrister and writer, became secretary of the Society of Authors. Shaw wrote to him from Ayot St. Lawrence.

2. Roberts replied that what Shaw described applied only if the author were resident abroad.

3. (George) Emlyn Williams (1905–87), Welsh-born actor who played Snobby Price in the *Major Barbara* film, was also a dramatist. In 1937, MGM filmed his play *Night Must Fall* (1935).

[Advice on Gabriel Pascal's Financial Arrangements]

(P/TL to Marjorie Deans, 3 August 1943/DHL)[1]

Mr Rank has sent me the names of the directors of his Company: Leslie Farrow and Viscount Margesson.[2] It could not be better; and I have sent him a draft agreement for St Joan.[3] This agreement secures to Gabriel the artistic direction of the film, but leaves him in every other respect to take care of himself. This he is quite incapable of doing; so you must take care of him. He must now make a very careful agreement with Rank's company for his services as art director: in fact he should have a printed form for this, as I have, with space at the end for additional clauses peculiar to each occasion. This should be for a professional fee for the entire production, payable at so much per week until the delivery of the completed negative, when the balance should be paid in a lump sum. Thus it becomes his interest to complete the work in as short a time as possible. The company must be bound to put down a stated sum to cover the production, Gabriel undertaking to keep within this limit.

This professional fee for artistic work gives the company no claim to any other activity on his part. For instance, he has gone to America to negotiate the American distribution. This is no part of his business: he has rushed into it quite thoughtlessly; and the only reason for his employment as commercial traveler, which is not his job, is that he is *persona grata* with the British Treasury on the one hand and known to the American firms on the other. He cannot settle anything until the agreement with me is executed, and he is authorized formally by the company to represent it in the U.S.A. He can ascertain the best distributors to choose IF the necessary agreement goes through.

Now it is in respect of this extra service that he can claim a royalty on the receipts, with the proviso that if he exceeds the estimated cost of the production the excess shall be deducted from the royalty, as proposed in the present case. But of course he can in his general practice make the royalty part of his remuneration as artistic producer, and decline absolutely to meddle in the business of finance at all. In any case this had better be left to the special clauses to be typed in at the end of his printed standard agreement when (if ever) he has one. It is intolerable to have to draft afresh every time a string of clauses which should be in every agreement he signs.

When you have taken this in, keep it at the back of your mind; for it is no use talking to Gabriel about it. He is much cleverer than the business people; but as he is not interested in business whereas they are interested in nothing else all the time, their interests will always be attended to and his neglected unless he has a vigilant and devoted keeper.

Bear in mind that as I must die presently he must not think of the situation as one for a gentleman's agreement between friends, but as one in which I shall be represented by the Public Trustee, who must insist on the strict fulfilment of all legal obligations. That is why under my draft agreement Gabriel incurs no financial obligation to me whatever. He has done everything in his power to entangle himself (he is dreadfully entangled over Barbara); but I have defeated him and left myself entirely free as far as I am concerned. Dont let him use his freedom to entangle himself seven times worse with somebody else.

Faithfully

G. Bernard Shaw

1. Written at Whitehall Court.

2. J. Arthur (later Baron) Rank (1888–1972), head of the Rank Organisation, was a titan of the British film industry. Leslie William Farrow (1885–1978) was a chartered accountant who served in several wartime offices, including the Ministry of Supply. Henry David Reginald Margesson (1890–1965), first viscount of Rugby, was secretary of state for war in Winston Churchill's first cabinet.

3. In the event, the Rank Organisation produced *Caesar and Cleopatra*, not *Saint Joan*.

[Trade Unions and the Running Time of Movies]

(X/TL to Gabriel Pascal, 25 September 1944/*SP*)[1]

Now to business. First, as to the dispute with the trade unions. If Independent Producers, instead of sticking to its business of producing, is going to engage in the class war with its extras, and make friction when it should be making films, then I shall rule it out of my future arrangements. I prefer oil to sand in my bearings. Extras who do not belong to a union and will not join it, are, in the lump, stupid, disloyal, selfish, undisciplined vagabonds. Those who belong to a union are sensible, provident, steady, punctual, and can be disciplined by their union if they behave unreasonably. The war between employers and trade unionists is a hundred years out of date. Urge Arthur to make it a rule at once that no extras shall be employed by him unless they belong to their union. Let him make another rule that if there are any grievances he must not be troubled with *ex parte* [one-sided] individual complaints; but they must be brought before him by the union secretary. This will at once put an end to the present friction, delay, expense, and distraction, and improve the quality of the personnel at Denham.

An employer who is not a member of an employers' federation is a fool. So is an employee who is not a member of a trade union.

Second, there must be an end of this funk about the length of the film. If films are to be restricted to two hours to please the one horse cinemas who must have two features and a slapstick comic to make up their programs then we must at once scrap Cæsar and rule out Saint Joan with all my major works which run for three hours, and fall back on Arms and the Man, Androcles, and the like. Cæsar is hardly long enough for a one-feature program; and the first condition we must impose on the exhibitors is that Cæsar-plus-a-newsreel must be the whole and sole program, and the occasion marked as a very special one, possibly even by doubling the charge for admission. Any other policy will only confirm Hollywood in its conviction that Shaw is a detrimental author. That was what made United Artists sabotage Barbara.[2]

G. Bernard Shaw

1. Written at Whitehall Court.

2. They sabotaged it by cutting its running time from 121 to 115 minutes when it opened in America and by cutting it 15 to 25 minutes more when it went to local cinemas.

Cæsar and Cleopatra

(C/X/QI/*Photo World*, February 1945)

PHOTO WORLD: It is notable that in common with others of your plays, Cæsar and Cleopatra in its original form had such ample stage directions as almost to be a [film] scenario in itself. What other plays of yours do you think would make good films if treated on the lines adopted for filming Cæsar and Cleopatra?

SHAW: All good plays make good films. The notion that there is any difference between the art of the playwright and that of the filmwright is a superstition from the days when the screen was dumb and the cinema was "the pictures," not the drama. But the difference in physical and financial conditions is enormous. The staging of Cæsar in 1898 cost £2000 ($10,000): the screening of it has already cost more than £200,000 (a million dollars). . . .

PHOTO WORLD: This film will probably reach American audiences. It has been said that the average mental age of American movie audiences is twelve; do you think they are able to benefit by seeing your film?

SHAW: It will certainly reach American audiences. All audiences today are politically infantile: but here again you are out of your depth in classical art. As soon as children can read they can be given The Pilgrim's Progress, the Bible stories, Dante, Homer, and Shakespear long before the day's newspaper would be intelligible to them. You need not fear that the Cæsar film will be too sophisticated for American or any other audiences. If my works did not appeal more or less to all ages I should have to renounce my claim to be a classic. I am afraid you under-rate my pretensions.

What I Think about the Film Industry

(QI/*Daily Film Renter*, 1 January 1946/IR)

What in your opinion is the future of the cinema?

I know nothing about the future.

If you had your time over again would you write for the screen rather than for the stage?

Yes.

What is your opinion of Hollywood's treatment of plays as compared with that of British producers?

I do not concern myself with Hollywood. I write for America, a quite different country.

Where in your opinion do the Hollywood and British producers go wrong? In other words, what do you suggest would be the ideal technique of producing motion pictures?

I am sorry, but I cannot take you on as an apprentice.

What do you notice chiefly in British pictures as (1) a shining virtue, (2) a glaring defect?

Whose British pictures? Mine and Gabriel Pascal's or So-and-so's?

Do you think that the enormous popularity of the kinema has been a benefit to the stage? Has it tended to make people more drama-conscious, and so lured many into the flesh and blood theatre who might not otherwise have gone?

Yes, of course it has.

What was your opinion of Henry V?

Quite interesting to theatrical antiquaries as a peep behind the scenes and before them in Shakespear's day. But you cannot have a play if you destroy the illusion of the stage; consequently no Henry V.[1]

Is the propagandist value of the pictures as great as is claimed for it?

Much greater. The world wars were largely Hollywood products.

What would you suggest as the next best advance in kinema technique?

Whats wrong with the present technique? It is good enough for anyone who can master it and is a born playwright. The others should peddle baked potatoes.

Can you envisage a time when screen drama will be able to devise its own plots, and so become independent of novels and plays?

There is nothing to prevent its doing both at present except simple incompetence.

Is Saint Joan going to be filmed?

Yes.

Which of all your plays do you regard as the most suitable for filming?

All good plays are suitable.

Have you anything printable to say about the average movie on which the fortunes of the industry have been built up? We dont mind what it is.

There is no such thing as the average movie. In fine art there is always trash, mediocrity, and treasure. Some of the movies are better than many of the talkies. But drama in its highest reaches cannot exist without speech. When, as at present, there is practically no limit to scenic, vocal, and financial possibilities, or to magnification, illumination, and audibility, the film leaves the stage nowhere. But that does not prevent the Punch and Judy man from earning a living.

1. Laurence Olivier begins his *Henry V* film (1944) with the camera moving from a view of London in Shakespeare's day to backstage and then onstage at the Globe Theatre, where actors in obvious makeup and costumes enact the play before actors playing Shakespeare's audience. When the play's action moves to France, the film changes to illusionistic realism.

[The Need for Adaptation to a Different Medium]

(X/TL to Peter Watts, 3 October 1946/CL 4)[1]

Do not treat my printed text with blindly superstitious reverence. It must always be adapted intelligently to the studio, the screen, the stage, or whatever the physical conditions of performance may be.
          G. Bernard Shaw

1. Written at Ayot St. Lawrence. From 1941, Peter Michael Watts (1900–72), formerly an Old Vic stage manager, was a BBC producer.

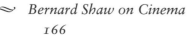

[Should a Theatre Company Produce Talking Films? (II)]

(P/HL to Gabriel Pascal, 18 November 1946/Del)[1]

I am entirely against this. The theatre and the cinema are quite distinct businesses, and must be kept separate. The proposed attempt to combine them would ruin the Theatre Guild or convert it into a common commercial film company. Let it stick to its proper job. It must come as far as I am concerned.

G. B. S.

1. Written in red ink on an undated carbon copy of a TL from the Theatre Guild to Pascal, in which the Theatre Guild proposed the formation of a joint company organized for it to produce Shaw's plays, which Pascal would then film. Compare Shaw's letter to Lawrence Langner, 15 February 1930.

In the Balance: Memo to Hollywood from Bernard Shaw

(C/*Screen Writer*, October 1947)

In economic principle the seventyfive percent British tax on American movies is vulgar Protection, to which a nation so inveterately Protectionist as the U.S.A. cannot consistently object.

But as national affairs in the U.S. and the British Commonwealth are managed by politicians who have no political principles at all, only habits and interests, this point is academic. The 75 percent tax is in fact one of the desperate expedients to reduce the export of dollars to which the British government is being driven by the immediate pressure of events.

For its effect on American film production nobody outside Hollywood gives a rap; and anyhow, nobody knows.

If Hollywood would add to its technical proficiency some evidence of higher morality than that of dealing with villainy by a sock on the jaw from the virtuous hero, it would make its films indispensable everywhere.

As it is, Hollywood is largely responsible for two world wars.

G. B. S. and Charlie

(C/QI/*Cavalcade*, 6 December 1947)

Are you still of the opinion that Chaplin is the screen's only genius?

Nobody is the ONLY genius. Mr Chaplin, no longer Charlie, is probably one of the best half-dozen.

Do you prefer Charlie the Crusader to Charlie the Tramp?

I have not seen his latest film.[1] He lost nothing by the change: gained by it, in fact, as he could not go on tramping forever.

Do you accept Charlie's theory that murder is sanctified by numbers, so that the State accepts a general as a hero and condemns the small killer as a villain?

He has put forward no such theory. Do you suppose that Shakespear is committed to the views of Caliban, or Molière to the morals of Don Juan?

How would you like Charlie to direct a film of one of your plays?

Rather. But he would be better employed directing one of his own.

1. *Monsieur Verdoux* (1947).

Bernard Shaw Is Fan of Chaplin

(C/*Sunday Pictorial*, 11 January 1948)

[Chaplin is a genius but is not] a damned fool politically.

Who is not "up against modern society" after fourteen years of murder and destruction?[1]

Chaplin is still the same great artist: a tragic clown, though the baggy trousers are worn out.

1. In 1947, the House Committee on Un-American Activities began hearings on the influence of Communists in Hollywood. It indicted ten Hollywood fig-

ures; and the Screen Directors Guild banned Communists from holding office. The dawn of what would be called McCarthyism began. Although Chaplin explicitly stated that he was not a member of the Communist Party or any other political party, Red-baiting pressure groups intensified a smear campaign against him and succeeded in limiting the circulation of *Monsieur Verdoux*. In 1952, he began a self-imposed exile from the United States and did not return for twenty years.

Rules for Directors

(X/*The Strand*, July 1949//ST)

Modern direction includes film direction, in which there is no limit to scenic possibilities; and directors may spend millions of pounds profitably instead of a few thousands. The results so far include megalomaniac demoralizations, disorganization, and waste of time and money. These evils will cure themselves. Meanwhile, the art of the playwright and director remains basically the same. The playwright has to tell a good story, and the director to "get it across."

[The Application of Shaw's Policy to a Legal Problem]

(P/TL to Ercole Graziadei, 24 January 1950/Del)[1]

Learned Sir,

It is not possible for me to make all the changes your clients desire. I know that in film business the Distributors get the lion's share at the expense of the Producers and Authors. They shall not get it at mine. My percentage is on what the Exhibitors pay to the Distributors. I have the monopoly and it is for Producers to bargain accordingly with the Distributors.

I never sell my rights: I retain them all intact, and proceed by licensing their exploitation. My licence is never for the world but always for the language only. For example, Clause 4 leaves me free to license native production in any country except Italian. There must be no dubbing. It is my policy to encourage native film production and prevent its being barred by foreign films, especially American ones.

If I were to wait for my royalties until the production expenses were recouped I should be making a profit sharing agreement with a speculator with no capital, which is quite out of the question in my case.

If your client cannot afford these terms I shall regret it, but shall have to dispose of Androcles elsewhere; for if I alter them for one I must alter them for all.

If they are accepted I will send you a separate agreement for the Italian language.

       Always yours with my best consideration
       G. Bernard Shaw

1. Written at Ayot St. Lawrence. Gabriel Pascal was negotiating with Count Ercole Graziadei (b. 1900), a Roman lawyer who was head of Nuovo Rinascimento (New Renaissance) Films, to produce *Androcles and the Lion*. Shaw sent a contract licensing rights in the English language only. Because Italian law demanded that if a picture were produced in Italy in English, Pascal told him, it must also be produced in Italian, and he pleaded with Shaw to add Italian-language rights. Shaw devised an ingenious solution to the conflict between his one-language-only policy and Italian law. Because of its unusual formality, perhaps attributable to Pascal's example or suggestion as to the customary mode of correspondence with this recipient, Shaw's salutation is included.

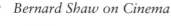

Appendix

Index

Appendix

Sample Licence for Film Rights

(P/Del)[1]

MEMORANDUM OF AGREEMENT made this   day of   between GEORGE BERNARD SHAW of Ayot Saint Lawrence in the County of Herts (hereinafter called the Author) of the one part and

(hereinafter called the Licensee) of the other part whereby it is declared and agreed as follows: —

WHEREAS the Author being the sole owner of a play (hereinafter called the Play) written by him and entitled has made or adopted a talking film scenario of the same and whereas the Licensee proposes to make a talking cinematographic film of the said scenario (hereinafter called the Film) in the   language and to dispose of it and reproductions thereof for commercial exploitation and public exhibition. NOW THIS AGREEMENT WITNESSETH that the conditions on which the said proposed transaction may take place are as follows: —

1. The Author enters into this Agreement not only for himself but for his executors administrators and assignees.

2. Subject to such limitations and changes (if any) as are or may be imposed by law on the Author's rights he authorizes the Licensee by way of Licence of the period of[2]   ending the[3] day of   nineteen hundred and   and from the date of this Agreement until the end of the current year to make and reproduce a talking film of the said scenario and to dispose of reproductions thereof as set forth above during the said period.

3. The Licence granted in the preceding Clause Two is peculiar to the Licensee and whilst empowering the Licensee to authorize exhibitions of the Film directly or through employed distributors is not assignable nor negotiable nor in any way transferable.

4. In all contracts made and transactions effected under this Agreement for the exhibition of the Film which impose on the exhibitor any obligation to exhibit or accept or purchase for exhibition any other film or batch of films this Film shall be separately accounted for at its own peculiar value.

5. In any foreign neighborhood with a resident speaking population numerous enough to maintain picture theatres in which it is assumed that the native language of the audience is the films manufactured under this Agreement may be exhibited in such theatres but no such film shall without the express consent of the Author be made intelligible by translation inscription commentary or otherwise to anyone unacquainted with the   language it being fully understood between the parties hereto that the Author has licensed or may hereafter license the manufacture and exhibition of films of the Play in other languages under similar limitations.

6. The Film shall be completed and released for exhibition not later than the   day of   nineteen hundred and and if thereafter it should fall out of circulation or cease to produce a revenue for the Author for twelve months or longer then all obligations of the Author to the Licensee under this Agreement shall cease.

7. The Film shall follow the agreed scenario without transpositions interpolations omissions or any alterations misrepresenting the Author whether for better or worse except such as the Author may consent to or himself suggest but changes imposed on the Licensee or exhibitors by local public censorships or national laws shall not be deemed a violation of this clause.

8. The Author hereby warrants that he is the sole owner of the Copyright in the Play and declares that he has not by assignment licence or otherwise granted to any person firm or company other than the Licensee any cinematographic or talking picture rights in the Play in the

language in respect of the said period of and undertakes not to do so whilst this Agreement remains in force but in view of the possibility of the extension with his consent of the foregoing Clause Five he has disclosed to the Licensee that his contracts with his authorized foreign translators may in such event oblige the Licensee to use their authorized translations and to employ the said translators (should they desire such employment) to translate such passages in the scenario as are not in their authorized translations.

9. The Licensee undertakes that the Film shall be handsomely produced with the best available cast and that no unusual methods of advertizing it shall be employed or sanctioned by the Licensee without the knowledge and consent of the Author.

10. The Author or his representatives shall retain intact and continue to exploit in competition with the enterprises of the Licensee or otherwise all rights in the original play including for instance the licensing of direct theatrical performance televisions and broadcasts and excepting only the right with which this Agreement is specifically concerned but the Author shall not exercise his literary copyright to hinder the Licensee from such multiplication of copies of the scenario or parts thereof as may be needed for work in the studio.

11. The Author guarantees that the aforesaid Play contains no plagiarisms nor hidden slanderous allusions to individuals nor any features not apparent to the Licensee which could subject the Licensee to legal pursuit or hindrance other than that of censorship official or unofficial recognized or acted upon by public authorities in control of exhibitions and entertainments.

12. The Licensee may take any necessary steps to establish and maintain the Author's rights as proprietor of the scenario and take any proceedings which may be reasonably necessary to restrain any infringement of such rights and the Author hereby authorizes and empowers the Licensee to institute and prosecute such proceedings and take such steps as may be proper and expedient to protect such rights and to recover damages for their infringement and undertakes to give the Licensee all reasonable assistance and information in such action and the Author's

claim (if any) to a share of such damages shall not exceed half of the net sum realized by the License after payment of the actual legal costs.

13. The names of the Author in their customary professional form of Bernard Shaw (not George Bernard Shaw) shall be clearly shewn at the beginning of all films made under this Agreement and shall appear in all programs advertisements and appropriate publicity matter issued or controlled by the Licensee in this connection and no such publicity matter shall state or suggest that the authorship of the Film has been shared by any person whether employed or not in its manufacture.

14. Should the Licensee enter into any Agreement whatsoever in relation to the Film[4] with any party firm or company whomsoever between whom and the Licensee there is any financial interest direct or indirect by the one in the undertaking of the other or any partner or director common to both then such party firm or company shall as between the Author and the Licensee be deemed to be the employed agent of the Licensee with whom alone the Author is concerned under this Agreement.

15. In the event of the Licensee ceasing to carry on business or passing a resolution to wind-up or becoming subject to a winding-up order the aforesaid Licence with all obligations of the Author to the Licensee under this Agreement shall thereupon cease.

16. If the Licensee shall at any time wilfully fail to comply with any of the terms or conditions of this Agreement the Author may forthwith notify the Licensee of such default if it be remediable and of his intention to cancel this Licence if within a sufficient time after the date of such notice the Licensee shall not have made good such default and if the default be irremediable the aforesaid Licence with all obligations of the Author to the Licensee under this Agreement shall without notice forthwith cease.

17. On the termination of this Licence by expiration of the time limit or otherwise all manufacturing exhibitions and other powers whatsoever granted by or under this Agreement shall cease and revert to the Author

absolutely (but without prejudice to the rights of the Author to retain any money which has already been paid to him or to recover any which has become or may thereafter become payable to him under this Agreement or to sue for damages for any breach thereof) and[5] all negatives positives prints and reproducible copies of any description of the said Film made under this Agreement and then extant and usable shall become the property of the Author.[6]

18. Any notice remittance account statement scenario or other like matter which is required to be or may be given furnished or submitted under this Agreement by the one party to the other shall be given furnished or submitted by registered post addressed to the party at the address aforesaid or at such other address as may from time to time be notified by such party to the other party for this purpose and any such notice remittance account statement scenario or other matter shall be deemed to have been given furnished or submitted on the date on which the same was so addressed and posted.

19. In consideration of the Licence herein contained the Licensee shall pay to the Author or his accredited representative executors administrators or assignees a royalty of[7]   per centum of the gross sums paid by exhibitors to the Licensee or to any distributor renter or other intermediary between the Licensee and the exhibitors in respect of the Film and in the event of the Licensee acting as exhibitor the royalty to be paid to the Author in respect thereof shall be   per centum of the gross moneys received from the public for admission to every such exhibition at which the Film is shewn.[8]

21. The Licensee shall on every twentyfifth day of March and twentyninth of September following the release of the Film furnish to the Author a statement of account shewing the royalties due to him up to the preceding thirtyfirst day of December and thirtieth of June with particu-

lars of the receipts on which the royalties are calculated and all necessary figures as to the currencies and rates of exchange in and at which there have been credited and shall therewith pay to the Author at his British address or to his duly authorized agents or bankers.[9]

22. The Licensee shall keep complete records accounts and vouchers of all matters relevant to the exploitation of the Film including copies of all relevant agreements made by the Licensee and such documents shall be accessible to the Author or his duly authorized agents at reasonable times for inspection and verification.

23. If at the expiration of the term of this Agreement both parties should desire to continue as before any subsequent transactions between them in respect of the Film shall be governed by this Agreement *mutatis mutandis* subject to[10]   notice of termination by either party.

24. The manufacture of the Film shall be under the supreme artistic direction of[11]   who shall choose the cast in agreement with the Author and whose peculiar talent is of the essence of this contract and should the said   be unable or unwilling to undertake or continue the work the operation of Clause One of this agreement shall be suspended until the Licensee and the Author are agreed on the choice of   substitute or successor.

25. Neither the Film nor the advertisements thereof shall make any statement or suggestion that the supreme artistic direction of the Film by   has been divided or shared with any other person or persons.[12]

AS WITNESS OUR HANDS this   day of   nineteen hundred and

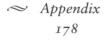

WITNESS to the signature of

....
....
....

WITNESS to the signature of

....
....
....

1. Shaw had other licenses with minor variations. Significant differences will be cited in footnotes.

2. In this clause and in clause 8, "five years" is invariably written by hand.

3. In this clause and in clause 6, "thirtyfirst" and in the next space "December" are invariably written by hand.

4. Some licences contain the phrase "in relation to the distribution of the Film."

5. In some licences, the remainder of the clause reads differently: "the Licensee shall forthwith render to the Author a statement of all available negatives positives prints and reproducible copies of any description of the said film made under this Agreement and the Licensee if so required by the Author shall destroy or cause to be destroyed all such material and shall produce to the Author satisfactory evidence of such destruction."

6. Some licences add this clause: "The Licensee undertakes to notify the time limit of this Licence or any extension of it to every party firm or company with whom they may contract in relation to the exploitation of the aforesaid license and the conditions of this Agreement shall in so far as applicable be made conditions of every such contract."

7. Here and in the next space, "ten" is invariably written by hand.

8. A space follows, in which a special clause 20 may be inserted.

9. A space follows, in which special conditions might be inserted.

10. In some licences, "six months'" is printed in the blank space; if not, "six months'" is invariably handwritten.

11. The name of the producer or director may be inserted in this blank space

and the next, as well as the blank space in clause 25. The third space in clause 24 is blank so that "his" or "her" may be inserted, as applicable.

12. A space follows so that one or more additional clauses may be added. On a licence to Pascal for a film of *The Shewing-up of Blanco Posnet* in Spanish, for example, Shaw handwrites a definition of the language as clause 26: "the so-called Castillian Spanish and not the Catalan dialect."

Index

Bernard F. Dukore, University Distinguished Professor Emeritus of Theatre Arts and Humanities at Virginia Polytechnic Institute and State University, has written or edited over thirty books and more than a hundred articles and contributions to books on drama, cinema, and dramatic criticism. Among them are works on Bernard Shaw, notably *Bernard Shaw, Director*; *Bernard Shaw, Playwright*; *The Collected Screenplays of Bernard Shaw*; *Money and Politics in Ibsen, Shaw, and Brecht*; and *The Drama Observed*, a four-volume collection of Shaw's drama and theatre criticism. They also include two books on Harold Pinter, two on Peter Barnes, one on Alan Ayckbourn, and *Dramatic Theory and Criticism*.